I Came, I Saw

Also by John Peck

Shagbark (1972)
The Broken Blockhouse Wall (1979)
Poems and Translations of Hi-Lö (1993)
Argura (1993)
Selva Morale (1995)
M and Other Poems (1996)
Inizia: Poems Yoked at Yuletide (2001)
Collected Shorter Poems 1966–1996 (2003)
Red Strawberry Leaf: Selected Poems 1994–2001 (2005)
Contradance (2011)

John Peck

I Came, I Saw

Eight Poems

Shearsman Books

Published in the United Kingdom in 2012 by
Shearsman Books Ltd
50 Westons Hill Drive
Emersons Green
Bristol BS16 7DF

Shearsman Books Ltd Registered Office
30–31 St. James Place, Mangotsfield, Bristol BS16 9JB
(this address not for correspondence)

www.shearsman.com

ISBN 978-1-84861-213-6

Copyright © John Peck, 2012

The right of John Peck to be identified as the author of this work
has been asserted by him in accordance with the
Copyrights, Designs and Patents Act of 1988.
All rights reserved.

Acknowledgments:

My thanks to the following editors and their journals:

Robert Archambeau, *Samizdat* (1, Autumn 1998), *Past these four walls*, here movement eleven, *Intermezzo lento for solo viola*, in *I Came, I Saw*;

John Matthias, *Notre Dame Review*, "A Compound March" (reprinted permission of *PN Review*), a preliminary version of *An Unstruck Sound is the Initial Move*, and *On the Sentencing of Philip Berrigan, Portland, Maine, 1997;*

Michael Schmidt, *PN Review*, "A Compound March".

Brian Swann, *OnEarth* (NRDC), the *Beekeeper's boxes* segment of movement four, *Gavotta grotesche* in *I Came I Saw*; and the poem in epigraph, *July*.

For kind attention to the title poem at various stages, I wish to thank John Gittins, John Hopkins, Jock Ireland, and John Matthias. In 'Gull and Cairn', my translations from Bernanos have benefitted from versions by Pamela Morris, David Schindler, Jr., and R. Batchelor.

Cover: *Aindiyai I Kadzhi* (1972) by Levan Tsutskiridze,
by courtesy of the artist. All rights reserved.

Contents

Prelude: July	7
"An Unstruck Sound is the Initial Move"	9
From the most fruitful	20
Puppe: A Causerie	25
"A Compound March"	30
Gull and Cairn	38
Whaling City	42
On the Sentencing of Philip Berrigan, Portland, Maine, 1997	50
I Came, I Saw	59
Notes	116

To Levan Tstuskiridze, painter

and with tribute to three unsung, incompatible figures from mid-century last:

*Jan Byzcewski,
engineer, diplomat, and émigré*

*Helmut Toepfer,
engineer, one-eyed survivor of a Russian prison ship,
and émigré*

*Johannes Felbermeyer,
painter, archival photographer, amateur archaeologist,
and émigré*

July

The single juniper spearing through
the crest meadow: from our road today
it drifted the ramrod poise of a bodyguard
on the running board of a black limo.
Three goldfinches pulse and dip into pin oaks.
Already the evenings grow shorter.
A heli hammers past, its rotors winding in tackle,
its cadmium eye bleary wet.
The giant must have returned home by now.
Where did I put my knife?
Tulip, oak, maple, hickory: nothing moves.

"An Unstruck Sound Is the Initial Move"

> *The Logos is a dog.*
> —The *Phaenomena* of Aratus of Soli,
> after Eudoxus of Cnidus

    The argument,
while we flow through these slow-burning forms,
    is that mind
on fire nests in logic on fire and slow-sounding.

    And that logic
as logos, no trick of the hearted mind
    to sound it that way,
is flame strung beaded along combers of sound.

    At Seven Pines
a storm the previous night left high reaches
    of the air warmer.
Sound curved earthward. Baritones and basses
    at the nearby front
mouthed and bellowed into a dome of quiet,
    even the squealing
mortars. And so General Joe Johnston
    heard nothing of that
and paced waiting, then galloped to it at night
    shot from the saddle.

When finally you hear it, the beat comes on
    steadily, a long
concourse in flood, unvalved river.
    When you attend to it
totally, it is the total, roaring at ease.

    Sebastian Bach
soprano to bass set out the registers
    where the fight throws them,
a plane otherwise mingled and confused,
    esprit gloom joy *fides,*
and dangles them out into speech, ropey cataract
    down to rock swaying.

    And in their stepped
separations I hear slowness although
    the years hasten,
bond enlarging throughout the speeding whole.
    His chorus barks
for death, then in chorale measuredly
    laments that and makes
peace with itself through sound wider than mind.

But past a feeling carried all the way out
    curves the domed full
    limit bellied
in wind thrown bellied by fire, sheeted fast
    to the rail heeled
over in running seas, and it hums, all going.

    He spread past any
single voice in the chorus, or choice foursome,
    though here among tents in the
clearing come only these calls he gave them after
    the storm's passing.
The jerky recitative of his gospeler—
    it spikes and buckles,
then bleeds repose, space opening and salved,
    one German spreading
through it to the skull's rim past Arcturus,

      most lucid sleep,
the skull itself great fountain and great bowl
      and he up its plume,
trajected among swift stillnesses.
      In the small hours
I hear the gurgle crowning that column, I've seen
      a sail curve space.
The bony campaign cup of the footsloggers
      in sutured calcium
is Euclid's father and the rim of peace.

      And mother's domed mother:
dementia rippled from it, a soggy veil
      across her blanked brow,
when my name, finding, went in, her face a caress.

      So: it lies everywhere?
This matte architecture of the dreamed
      and yielded blood,
humps of it tilting from the fields? So: it
      tents, pitches up, sinks?

The technical college built for the children
      of Polish immigrants,
brick colonial, now a prison for women,
      browed the hill over town,

Kościuszko naming one of those halls,
      the émigré to Paris
who studied painting and then as extern haunted
      the military academies
imbibing engineering and the *philosophes*.
      Thus in Virginia

he both painted Jefferson in laurelled profile
    and talked *les droits de l'homme*.

Kościuszko! But Andrei Tadeusz
    also lived in the house,
the genius engineer who whitened
    his thumbs' knuckles
by tucking each nail under and squeezing hard,
    having been enrolled
an R. O. T. C. lieutenant
    of engineers, infantry,
a saber with his name etched on it
    in the upstairs closet,
swayback blade and basket hilt in the years
    when Spain was taken, then Poland
and stiff cardboard camp photos
    of lubberish pontoons
on, it might have been, Meade's Rappahanock
    when Faulkner was cranking up *Hamlet*
for reruns in Yoknapatawpha
    (*Hamlet! why I could write that*),
his unit snapped up at Corregidor
    while he pulled steel furnaces
from the sleeve and tungsten of Oz,
    and a sheath for Alamogordo—
Washington wrote him a gilded reference
    but the Czar locked him up:

bastions, angles of fire, the calculus
    of materiel filtered through calendars,
cobbling together an uprising (betrayed)
    while the state here
commenced morphing into max density,
    growth minus magnesium
in the bones, and steel alloys accordingly,
    a state without citizens

and the fortress bulked out past reason
    or salient, the salient
reasons seeping into crapulous treasuries,
    bilious bodies.

The figure bobbing in grease-monkey's cap
    and red lumberjack shirt
between ranks of orange tiger lilies
    was my Tadeusz, alias Clarence,
who cleared the back of the cement-block garage
    so that I could string up
my perpetual-motion rig (building the entire
    industrial heating division,
he then bought the one house in that village
    which sat next to a manure pile,
on his shelf among the manuals his dog-eared
    Five Acres and Independence by Bromfield)

and of course explained that energy is conserved through
    system loss, *non perpetuum*
but still supplied the gear and said we would then
    see how it actually worked.

The division was undone in one year by a pet
    of the company's top bosses.
As was Kościuszko at Ticonderoga,
    spotting Sugar Loaf Mountain
near the great fort and advising St. Clair, in vain,
    to put a battery up there.
Came total rout. I extracted 18th-century spectacles
    from the back-yard garden,
Connecticut puritans having plowed there
    when it was their Northwest,
whose children would do business one day

     at John Brown's nearby tannery—
no insurgent he, roared safe Wendell Phillips,
     no, Brown checked moral entropy,
the impersonator of God's law, an orator's dream,
     a regular Cromwellian
dug up from two centuries, the very flywheel
     of perpetual renewal.
Kansas the back of *that* garage, *goods without guilt,*
     Canaan with Cromwell and Valley Forge,
energies compacted whirling self-renovating,
     Pastor Higginson exulting
War only educates men to itself, then Quantrill
     nine years later burning Lawrence
and slaughtering 183 unarmed men and boys.
     Yet the thermodynamic lesson
ends with possession of the land. *The race to accumulate,*
     Canaan a plump tale:
the temples on those gunmetal eyeglasses slid,
     shafts through tabby yokes,
like so many laced arms in a hoe-down after harvest,
     happy change of partners.

     Eight years earlier
Clarence Peck was at Los Alamos, Alamogordo,
     testing the sheath formula
in explosions it was meant to contain, and did.

     Not motion unending
but force turned back on itself to trigger
     all hell throughout hades
(the chains rattling and breaking in plutonium)
     high in *heofenes*
(veiled, *sacer,* yoked in *temenos,*
     havoc in the forecourts
to kindle altars in the *sanctum nucleatus*)

the man with a hoe shaking the tall orange lilies
    and getting them to grow
when others with chemical finesse got nowhere,
    veiled from his own kin

and a sealed secretariat at his own hearth,
    separated out:
himself the secretion of capacity into desert *secretum*
    so as to declare **o p e n**
the super-dense halls and enclaves of Seaborg's
    Element 94,
heaviest of the primordials, saying, *Fling wide*
    at the beck of my alloy steel jacket
when the love that he sacrificed, her form
    nowhere in view, lay
as blood across freshly plowed furrows
    through a field (Brown's Pennsylvania
    or Brown's Kansas)
which crossed the field of my inner vision with sorrow
    at remembering that Bromfield's book
went with him wherever his moves took us.
    Many forms, the primordial
silvery white assumes the guise of allotropes
    directly under the gaze,
shifts through its subaltern states *cervus fugitivus*.
    Yet the hoe wiggling among curved stalks
and orange trombones, ice cream on the back stoop in June
    as he conducted with spoon,
Brahms on the cranked-up phonograph, windows wide,
    these stay clear of the whitish metal.
Not Lowell's dynastic peeling of the Boston onion
    nor his jail time as conshie
rolled out the poetics for this coeval chapter.
    Dirac's balsa glider and tight lips, perhaps.
    Thus, he with hoe, me with pulleys.
Every pastoral seals an epochal white-knuckler.

  Our seminar conversation at noon
concerned angular momentum, not Dante.
  *Here is where you must add
input* smiling *to keep your design going.*
  He lifted the sinker, my fail-safe,
which never rose quite as high the next cycle.
  The true white-knuckler prohibits
recollection, forestalls the pulley's rope gather, preoccupies.
  Over the desert that peculiar
luminosity doggedly perseverated in seared retinas.

His birthday gift that year was a dinner
  with his colleague R.
who brought his hand-made telescope and propped it
  in backyard drifts to pull in Venus,
colleague Helmut there, too, hired from '50s Germany,
  one eye and one good hand
(a prison ship in the Black Sea), the black patch a jest for French R.,
  all three men, I now sense,
in their turns at the cold eyepiece knowing relief
  at having been secreted there
safely, chatting about orbits, objective lenses—
  for *The Aesthetic Education of Man*
must include them also or else it stands prejudiced,
  include as well the former priest
who smartly blurted to me at the early café
  in a wintry Swiss city
Your president has just bombed Baghdad
  All precision, all snappy
as if playing an ace and leaving me with a full hand,
  that release of tension a coitus
as elemental as rape long threatened then sprung,
  bringing Venus in close
with her torn cloud, the stretch marks of unacknowledged births,
  all those worlds
deposited short of nourishment and futures

so that the posture of freshness
not examined too closely might still jive Mars.

When the division collapsed, Peck with two helpers
    worked at card tables for months
into the night, placing every man with cousin firms
    and rivals. So at their reunion
he was the other Kościuszko with diagonal sash
    and the *Virtuti Militari*,
an aura coming off his skin in the Sunnyvale
    sirocco: his men. His men.

The argument also is
    that an unstruck seeing
  goes blind, because deaf—
that the eye which has heard nothing cannot yet
    see to see. At one speed,
sight inside hearing, one riding the other
    into their bond
    in our white cup.
As hulking Orion tilts on one heel unfazed
    by the deep smear
of a meteorite down midriff and belt—
    the long return
was over, his pride and blindness composing him
    to shoulder a dwarf
who saw him home to the rising sun. For now
    fate was otherwise,
destiny had gone out in freedom among
    those lanes and endless
sparkings and not been seared or scarred further,
    the skull threw no more
Lutheran nights beyond itself but sped
    to the maximum
velocity of event here, sang, and floated,

      for all the damage
had been done. The doers were now no more
      than four scorable
tremors of the mind's heart of Deutsch
      rectified, rising.

      So the scout knife from Norway,
that gift with blond haft and thick fixed blade--
      to set roofing tar
my father took it, then gave it to his father
      for gutting fish.
So with most of my learning: the shine went under
      and the tool traveled.
But gone it teaches me to listen for rumors
      of the unsounded—
knowledge is never *now*, and the second learning
      waits just there. A Muskelunge
drooping his hand as, up the slit, swift gleamings,
      wide for all the answers
meant to remain unstruck—big saddle vacant
      as the crash stills.

As a splattered vee down the fast lane slides under,
      the contents thus of
one sack of Roman lime and Greek will
      to align columns
on the wild aperture, arrayed trunks opening,
      spilled from a van
and married to the rains. All at one speed.
      Yes, it is ersatz
prefab the stuff is destined for, yet porous
      and unmorose past it
the thing that I must build rises to grasp it.

  And were I still shooting
to meet it down that lane, the trowel-less hand
  of a great sower
swiping, flared flat, would rustle across the pale
  non-statistical
corsage of horizons, pinned there from no garden
  I ever asked for.
Yet I dug, planted. And have turned to face
that fire the Bushman tells us he hears
  ringing, the sun.

From the most fruitful
loam
in time, out into fitful
day-flashes

sex's wet fire
gating
each of us: there is more
to birth than beginnings,

or is it from rivered
joinings whose pour curling over
mossed spillways fits flush their full width
and sheens
the whole flow into froth
as if destined,

no thing the hours float upward
not warming as it nears texture and fact—
arriving glowing.
    May this have been so even for each sleeping
white bundle through the slot
to a wheel that swung it out of sight
under a pair of painted babies
curled smiling. Convent days,
cries of orphans

through long afternoons and the seasons,
the oblong women's courtyard now near a loud

playroom with portable
partitions, inflatables,

the biggest ones for punching
or just bouncing,
administrators from their offices
amiably at ease
crossing through the rough-cut
women's arcades—I had not
intended to spend the late day
at the Spedale
degli Innocenti, Florence's first
and the West's oldest

and all business. All
on fortune's wheel:

the *rota's* mission is to spin—
this is your rotation, *caro bambino*,
these thin columns and plain
courtyard are your diamond, that huge one
they call *the Orphan*.

Through your courtyard March winds
tremble the young lemons.

   On Carrara's sidings,
on Massa's, outsize cubes press the springs
low on flat cars,
drill marks from the blasting grooving
their chalks and grays. And listing on beams through grass
bergs await cranes. No wheel—
a thin iron road lines them
out for their start.

Those quarries
close under the peaks—there Buonarotti's
furies could cool
toward his patrons,
their delays or botchings of his commissions
settling as he scaled planks
with the crews—
in slings they rodded chinks
hammering sagely and wetting ropes
to ease strains in the loads, on ships
an old trick:

slow separations
from the massif
over midwife man at his visions
placental in stone.

In his first years
cut off from mother, he carved his Marys
gazing vaguely
away from the boy,
a suckling ignored along her body
though she holds him among her infolding
foothills.
   This your rotation!
      Yes, she spurns any shielding
of the twice-born,
the luckier ones
once they know that. For whoever gains
the larger family,
released from the smaller,
can carve in free possession, the fuller
affiliations nowhere fixed
yet everywhere
to be found, even among unwaxed
flaws in the block,

even the ones hidden
and thus ruining a long effort—
      his maddened
sledge bashing Christ's
slung thigh away
late in making that *pietà*
with cowled Nicodemus—

yet just here must run
correction,
like the passage from smooth to rough
in his block, deep in:
they had him rage,
the early biographers, out of their own
habitual rummage
through bald pathos
and that inveterate choice of blackmail
made by the less before those with more—
this time more
consistency: invention within sculpture

from what painting
had done, stretching and remassing
flesh for the slanting
view from below by seekers
approaching an altar. Consistent
even through

the valley zone
of Christ's
wrapped sex, where smooth shades rough
at the thigh join,
last creation
to leap out of it clean across

that gap with no motion
needed, the great
being
simply there *nunc stans* through
changed angle of sight—
a giant's torso
as his leg
vanishes under his mother
and they hang so,

not always but once
in this carry, the leg in under her dense
grief, the blurred

mask of her face
melting into
his lank thrown hair, veiled kiss
as at last she sees him.

Puppe : A Causerie

Mimostoria,
the distilled gesture,
cantastoria,
the song line of act,
sinuously puppet-like
through malign paralysis
they rupture the integuments
of fact: wriggly, impudent,
hoarse and breathy, lone
against the tree line
or a palisade of office towers,
and death toothsome,
and Yama of red rule,
and remote planets flagrant
in crêpe, wobbling and
sweeping with cloth wings
down pasture, mutely
they play out the word
of the gods: medieval
Agamemnon among Suits
and scythes, gore-freaked muslin
gust-rippled there, lolling and bending—they stride
stiltedly fabulous
and fey into nemesis,
even at parade
halt, as when a titanic mutant
shrugged, its puppeteer choking in harness.
I felt his itch, his sweat—and so
through him at last I look out
from all those things I had seen merely
as things, unpenetrated,
through their apertures
prodigiously prized wide,
and make for the cloud bleachers

and half-sunk suns
crumbling, reforming.

2

Lumbering downfield,
swaying with the tall pseudo-tonnage
of molded glue-soaked paper,
the man's streaky bulk,
jigged on poles beneath and behind,
wavered in identity between bouncer, thug,
and some former pol or salaried spook
penitent in ripe decomposition,
or the ashen firefighters waving away microphones,
wagging heads open-mouthed as they softly turned back
to the ground they had named, again, Zero.
Behind, a laundered white scarp
toppled through itself cleanly
laboriously upward.
Huge hunting horns and black streamers
from the group below indexed
both the wild chase and the morgue
while eye holes and gaping maw floated
phantoms of agency either behind the game
or well ahead of it.
The slow-motion brawl
of double agents, freelance provocateurs,
veiled sponsors and deep corruptors
goes only half-shrouded,
no *formlines and ovoids*
from the Haida persisting in the hands
of Mungo Martin, Bill Reid,
to inspirit a whole people's
animal true mask.
As churches in Lisbon were engulfed
and in Johnstown submerged,
as Pueblo Bonito baked empty in Chaco Canyon

under the sun it had tracked keenly,
the center both gurgles and parches.
Once that bulk had tottered past,
the pole up its back tenting its vast jacket
around a figment of pain,
the acknowledged identities eased their grip
on any powers, either of containment
or insinuation, and the bobbing mass could go
to incapacity as to
a long home. And recalled to me
how a male psychiatric nurse,
seated one Christmas in our clinic
at the round upstairs table beneath a chandelier,
took the pint angel noosed with a gold cord
near a dejected inmate, chuckled knowingly,
and hung it there by the neck.
           He, too, does it!
Weeks later the man had greatly improved.
The cone of light during that night watch
melted shock by tightening the matzoh edict:
This is my body.
As if the gagged shrieks in some offshore detention
achieved embouchure past inaudible lockdown,
inscrutable custom, law:
show me the body!
habeas corpus produce the body, divulge
the flesh in question.
Political scientist,
soul doctor, vanished colleague and puppet master,
now I know accommodation, but to the fit
of order within order
settling as belt, collar, and lace
in acknowledgment
of the webby crime.

3

The egg-crate car-parks,
as impermanent as the mills
in Gary and Pittsburgh,
none the less girdle
Pharoanic pylons or the four piers
of the old core, Mont Saint Michel:
here body becomes head,
hiving the chances for speed, weight, harm's aim,
Adams's praise for the Mount's
great hall transferring aptly:
in those vaults *warlike emotion*
stamped everywhere,
in every ray of light,
on the mass of every shadow.
In his rooms Kurt Schwitters
canted non-Euclidean angles and slabs
of creamy accumulation
out from the walls, burying
the saved world in Hannover.
Which was bombed flat
by the time he made it to Norway,
but they came after him there, so Elysium Two
slid off the cliff also—therefore
only in Ambleside did the last one
bulge and slope in the hut of Ignotus.
El Lissitzky torqued the squares
on graph paper into steepling motion,
asserting that with one pull
we can vault into the act hammering,
justice beautiful in the act.
But the German émigré had iced our hour:
Schwitters ein schwirrender Schwitzer
in the sweat lodge of the empires maintaining his cool
though they parked him in Camp Hutchison on the Isle of Man
where Hans Bach, his widow told me, recruited a string quartet

and where eleven-year-old Tom Cassirer, Tom told me,
heard them play but did not meet the architect of *Merzbau*.
No one quite met him
in the green isle. A self-interred *Wunderkammer*
cannot be quite of this world
where the bowels of the Rhine of the body
would chamber the surrendered boroughs, the appalled precincts,
populous but self-emptying—
the horns and glides of Charles Ives frame in music
what this does in concrete
while I feather the brake, drifting
past the huge eye ports, down through
the spiral conch of Venus
and the veil of Isis to access
neither ardor nor release,
but sleeve more and more into
the features of my face
turn by turn.

"A Compound March"

Place of the lion in evening;
situation of good in the shiver of its morning;
fact's healing salt; amber's ardor; march of unities;
forgiveness's silt; awe's ease.
Harbor of the shrike's plunge; jetty of welcome; port's rocking pause;
peace, a fire inwrapping; resurgence, a fire gone out;
the city, a compound march; old paint's rolled seams;
the republic, a quilt of equilibrations; a swung latch.
Home a tongue unthought of; the oil of action;
iron door on railed wheels rolling to one side; a burden carried;
hay in moist darkness; wing feathers; the first unvoicing and last unworking;
forgetting as gate, enablement the path.
A thing given; a swift fragrance; a hand;
anything in its own flame; a release.

2

Borrowed bore-word that reams on in, auguring—
speech, action, and thought its drill field
until speech, action, and thought give place
until strife gives place, *strife*
closed in the sod and flown in the current,
atomized in the surf of time-space that foams
all of it now, however jangling.
Until a sound stops I have not heard it
and prior to performance I cannot anticipate
the actual sound. William Steinberg—stone mountain—
stood leading, not his *grosses Orchester*,
but a jazz ensemble, and the surprise
calmed anguish, a treasure had vanished
hard to obtain yet he timed the cure, all thanks
to chrome-dome jive-master for all his numbers
their stream beginningless over its silent bed:

a commonplace yet summary anguish
yet here heavenly living
its curious rest in a fellowship
shooting right on through the food fights, *Let 'er rip*
Herr Händel wanting violins
while the monarch hankered after percussion and brass.
Beginningless in addressing a cure to the endless.
Slide on, oily Thames, under loop-diving gulls.

3

Slosh on, Potomac, Rappahannock, James
kings and tribes mingling, blood from brother armies
a trace element.
       Mirrored in wiggly smears
from the bridge, headlights overwrite the undercurrent
of tenderness, my shiny hard cell among
amber beads lining out under moon rise, each bulge
with an animal and etheric body
tranced afloat in half-crouch
hands and feet parodying the Shaker
gestures in their line dances
       Beulah encased
in gleaming fragility under the floating bright cinder
Beulah encapsulated and thrown
rim shot scattershot
       tracers slowly curving.
Tenderness for that trance movement
       for it enwombs
something incalculable even to itself
and labors with it repeatedly until climax.
The lonely only empire's vaunt
and warning to all the peoples
lofts over the effort
benedictus qui venit in nomine
over us sealed off from each other

and the question *How did I get here*
flickers up from the two-million-year-old
gut rhizome *You my vehicle my double.*

4

You have to see what they've done to me now! My neighbor
in her mid-eighties scuttled
to her writing desk. *Look, they're even
duplicating my handwriting!* Out her window
the wide lake calmed a prickle of sails.
*This exact copy of my own house, they built it
in France, on another lake with the same hills,
everything. And they've been keeping me here,
but now this: this   t e r r i f i e s   me.*
Her jagged scrawl terminated
midway through a grocery list.
George Oppen, who suffered the same though not
in the same way, urged that one word
we needed to understand was *u s* .
What we make of each other. And psyche,
she who shares him and her with me and you,
going to school, learning to parse the lists,
bending over her desk with wisps
of curl dangling or braids,
leaves the tablet and goes home.
Arranges for Mary B. to live in her *other house.*
Replicates the landscape, boats, handwriting.
Has us study the word *m i n e* .
Doubles the scene, unsettling it. For it intends this.

5

Borrowed bore-word is any of them I take
as a first term. But once inside its sound

I may double the sense of it
not with dictionary but through
hum and rumble. This is as old
as the Vedic *rishis* and fresh as surrender
to medicine past grasping
and manipulation. Intended
familiar meaning is the first house.
Aural body is the second, booming
through the first house and spreading
out over the yard and the lake and transecting
a boat's rippling jib as it stills and then tacks.
Though you make the sound, it leaves you and migrates
among all other bodies
and harbors in their wave-rove, their rocking at anchor
in readiness for departure,
a steady congress of non-ownership
buoying all the grabbing gestures,
percolating them, detaching them, transmitting
constantly, porously receiving.
Any word at all borrows from this store.
The Shaker conga lines scooped love from their hips,
the lower chakras, and shoveled it into the air
while around them, or among them, swayed the singers.

6

U s for the eskimau embraced walrus, whale,
pursuer molting into his quarry.
Compassion for their kill: skilled, harsh caring.
Their articulated harpoons ended
in a walrus-bone aileron glued to the shaft's butt,
some of them fluted as many as four times
to channel the air. I stared at one of these
retrieved by Alekseev from the dig at Ekven
on the Bering Strait: *Butterfly form*
reads the caption. *In der Form eines Schmetterlings.*

What lay there was a stealth bomber,
hungry engine ports hugging its body,
stubby wings swept back into tubes.
The two patterns wrestled each other, bone
amber and grave-crudded
wrapped into and through the gleaming terrible.
They designed the thing that destroyed our house
before they could dream it. The house I must leave shoulders
up through the murderous gravel of a mutant
and devout species, every
doubling within it dislodging me
that much more. Though it could also snare me
if I let it. Could harpoon me. If I let it.

7

The Sophiolotry of the nineteenth-century Russian
thinkers, and Raskolnikov's Sophia,
and the Church's dogma of Mary's assumption, follow
the Shaker Mother Ann Lee's
embodiment of Christ as woman,
that coming a second time but not as the first thing.
They took in Lincoln's war orphans
and dressed right on *technē* and dressed plainly.
Furniture kits their downstream spin-off
in the era of total war: oil and wax
finish or lacquer over medium stain,
rock maple. But such are the lees
from their liquor. They wanted the uncut wine,
highs coming from self-conquest, peace
from hard labor, family from no marriage.
There is only one Son of God. And then Mother.
Not some duplicate on a reservation
but the further thing. And that thing here.
She came one year before Lexington
leaving four small graves in the English midlands.

While Robert Gould Shaw packed corpses from Antietam
with charcoal for trans-shipment
Elizabeth Johnson watched Ann Lee
come into the room singing and touch her arm
and felt the whole *mana* of the *tremendum* flow through her body.

8

Though *While* spans seventy years:
six thousand dissenting dancers when war came.
More than itself body recalls, waits for touch
that tells, if it comes.
The *w e* who sang and moved in them were not *u s*
in any transparent sense.
Not the hot guilts that upheaved them—
yet a thing that rises before song from the cells
and blooded centers, remembering
what no one invents. Forget the asexual
commune that mass-produced seeds and sit where you are
and stand it. And stand *in* yourself.
See what moves and move with it.
Skopas of Thessaly hired Simonides
to chant a praise song at one of his banquets
and in his poem Simonides magnified not only big
Skopas but Kastor and Pollux, and so the host paid him
half his fee: *Get the rest from those twin gods!*
Then a messenger called him outside to meet
two men. No one, so he went on looking in the dark,
when the great hall collapsed. Simonides, shaken
yet finding that he remembered everyone there
and where they had sat, was able
to identify the bodies.

9

The body remembers? Wasn't it the chanter?
Tópoi, places at table, *topics*—the run of an argument—
thought, action, speech the node of the labyrinth,
are they not all tremor from the throat-heart,
the medial chakras? *Ann Lee entered the room singing....*
At the node of the labyrinth, a blur of crossings.
The Greek rhapsode drafted as Notary Public—
yet the pair he invoked, like the Germanic
twin gods of healing, and also
their sainted doubles Kosmas and Damian,
presided over Mary B.'s imprisonment
in a cloned dwelling as memory decomposed,
to begin separating her from what
perishes. Another house for the body
prior to that shaky memo / hand on the arm
as she sits next to you, then the power / a tap
on the shoulder from the messenger /
                —at the node
of Mary's impacted synapses, and out of the epileptoid
cantata in Mother, and in Simonides' choice of the twins,
a harmony of doublings, the hand of two powers
to one end, either dragged as Mary was
or willingly singing the incalculable
touch of it. Priority goes to sound
if you like—touch is not jealous. The two. And the one.

10

In Meetinghouses the two singing battalions of the sexes
faced, filed between, turned, counter-turned, circled
coiling, forearms lifting and falling in time. Which were first
lifted by sufferings. Which have scribed
diagrams of the movements. *En masse*
our bodies moved or were startled away

was it from them?—still moving, or startling away.
For piano steel guitar and in our time
the commissions are for things hammered, plucked, zing-stroked,
hand and string as in the beginning. Thus the zap-cording
of a small round sifting floor in curved space with requisite
winds, metals, percussion, harvestable woods, voltages,
impacts from asteroids, padded sticks, rosined hair,
alkalis, pressed oozes, sunned scarps and vibrating
columns of air, leafing and stripped stems, and the good
gone all among them, for death is not to be conquered and
touch would run up and down all the routes there.
                    Lease to me
agile memento of that hurry and the cry fleeing in it
for massed bodies bend only to what sounds from
the doubleness at play in hands, their salty whorls across
tensiles, sheet ivories, the arrayed natures, as the blind girl
bellowed *WATER* her hand in its pouring. Lease it to me.

Gull and Cairn

The film snaps and shears: irretrievable.
On the raised beach I have just photographed a large gull
perched near a cairn on the ridge
of smoothed rubble, massed Mesolithic,
a twenty-foot-high mound in pastel ovoids.
The crackling sound from my little box has not dislodged him.
Though I have never been to Jamaica
I recognize the policeman in dress whites on his rostrum,
sans arms and gloves, *sans* traffic, but ministerial, magisterial, miniature,
a cock-cupid of the colonial backwash, head swiveling in surveillance.
And when I look back
he vacates in a flapping M,V,M,V
collapsible and portable *I WILL-BE HOWSOEVER I WILL-BE*
on pumpkin dangling feet.
Hours later I scan that ridge for the crest cairn:
that pile gone, though no wind stirs.
Yesterday was the feast of Theresa of the child Jesus, virgin,
Thérèse de Lisieux, dead at twenty-four:
noting her feast day in Georges Bernanos, I find that today
is the harbor of winged guardians.
As our own reach fills an unseen envelope,
life living itself maximus, to its own edge—
so do outlines of a tight pile and a bird
still swim gin-slow in chromey blue over the stones.
Neither afterimage nor cenotaph:
learn not from memory
how to go to the perimeter of the territory
right up to the fence wire and lean on it, into prairie wind.
Tubercular agony hung *thick dark* over Thérèse
as she clung loyally to *l'amour* on that pitch path, drawn dear down.
The finished has gone, but the tremble of it trails,
the unfinished within the finished hives in us, heaves up, haloes.
Precisely here last year sat a pair in webbed folding chairs,
crossed feet as inverted commas, pinkish-white soles outward,

dark shades and Panamas above two tummy-propped yellow novels
side by side, *J A W S* and *J A W S* .
Manifestly trawling for Moby, cagily dredging for porn.
Whereas I went at Bernanos' stagey sermon
in honor of Thérèse de Lisieux—
head side-to-side over the congregated, bill clacking—
sixty-seven years ago, two before France fell,
about the two canonizations:
young Jeanne d'Arc one year after the Great War and Thérèse five,
a solemn warning and an even more serious sign
rumbled the moustachioed bird to the assembled,
Hurry up and become children again, that we may become children too!
At which something bristles, huffing at his hale paradoxes,
then leaves the stage empty.
In the blue spaces left by him and the cairn
electric current uncoils.
So I too had been after something else.
It can't be so very difficult.
You are just as anxious to save your skins as we are.
The stentor pretends to wade in from the non-congregation,
the mongrel diaspora, out of its nowhere-everywhere
an innocent enemy.
His tactic: to yell, *If it's ONLY a symbol, then to hell with it.*
The rafters, however, send back something else:
If it's NOT a symbol, then to hell with it!
Felled by strokes, Thérèse's father Louis staggered from his chair
and grabbed his rifle and angled into the infantry crouch.
The gull's outline holds steady, the envelope tautens
swirls of immeasurable depth, boiling marine.
Tight with his fine harangue, I sensed a finer, harder thing past it.
Unable to stand it in his own lukewarm crowd, Bernanos
climbed heated turbulence—
Don't tell us they came only to add a few finishing touches to the painting—
path-blocker and enforcer
squeezing the lectern, bulging silently to suck in breath;
at least he did not subject them
to the sudden second-person of his essay on Joan—

Ah, you saw her eyes slowly fill with shadows,
and when you appeared on the threshold,
you saw her first nudge of retreat
towards the wall, and the artless
self-defense of her little lowered head—
pew-smashing Yeshua absent from the sun-warmed corner,
his *No* the clarity of the criminal:
void frame for this carney mouthpiece contriving the Macaw of himself
alighting before the owners of a voltage they never use,
raucous for innocence he'd seen
fill the near spaces then vanish.
Twice I patrol that stretch but only the outlines swirl there
lucent as migraine patches in a stumbling eye,
not the Anglo-Saxon poet's brown-out
Cloud over God's body / Shadow went forth
but the intact graininess of poverty and magnanimity.
Sumbolon, the thrown thing, the sail of itself rippling out,
the arc of its lob steadied on a stone,
how is it gone if its wealth still populates its vacancy?
Gone to hell because someone hollers?
Twice those profiles,
while for one year and a half, light fled and heart nothinged
as she held fast:
Thérèse, *therizein*, harvester
harrowed and invisible, finishing as *J'aime Dieu!*
the hollowing out of love drawing it back more mightily
out of long dearth, a doorframe to its wiriest lines,
their fluent mesh weightless save to the wasting might
of her last grasp and outcry.
Incorruptible velvet, the black drawn blind.
Yet inexorable her quietly active acid
cherishing the grind, loving bitchy him or her, nicing the nasties.
How is it futile if it's never poured?
And twice, only those profiles
azure and accurate, the demand beyond them
alive, insistent vacant raiment
with a brave bird inside: unseen

unless I sit for the agony of simplification
that settles then fumes off on the crest of emergency.
A clear day in one more October through all that is
as heaped stones in their wave poise and pause.

Whaling City

—in memory, Emmett Jarrett,
the Third Order, Society of Saint Francis

On the back of his huge hand the skin,
roseate, shiny, nearly orange,
testifies not only to late-April chill in vagrancy
but also animation in his telling Pastor Emmett
about not quite identifying the half-frozen man.
Days ago, New London closed its homeless shelter.
Bill wanted me as moral support when he told the cops.
It was on the border with Waterford. That wan't no problem
though when them two sets of cops come Bill disappeared
and all I could say was "I don't know" but they kept astin' me.
A thick sweatshirt hood cowls his face at noon,
cornice on the gable of his portable house.
The stiff lay near the Thames down the embankment.
His hand was still on his heart, like he might've
had a attack while he was thinkin' of peein'.
The Waterford cops get out maps to see if he's theirs
and then ours get out t h e i r *maps. Pretty soon*
I see them give Bill a grinder and then he leaves,
and there I am without even no coffee!
The state first and last means territory.
Gertrude Bell's bath in Baghdad, a tin saucer on the floor,
invasion has ridged and rivered with red sand.
Joan unfurled her banner
to mark out ground for the homeless Dauphin.
Loved her sword less, but loved it: *Miserere nobis.*
Rosy Hand talks temperature and weather with Emmett.
Through a gap in nineteenth-century facades
the green General Dynamics Boat Shed looms over the estuary
like the blimp hangar at Sunnyvale in the '30s.
She ain't there no more, the U.S.S. Hawaii shot the slip last week.
I put in real work on her
so she went out and under, she of the subsurface world of tooth and trident,

longer than two of the sperm whales once hunted from here.
One vessel takes out six small countries.
The hand treads the boundary with singed tips
from Hesiod to Yeshua, yet denies it: borderline, uniter!
Out of guilt for Tokyo's blaze McNamara
aimed away from all the little houses toward bases.
Miserere! That stoked compunction hungers for a first strike.
A fire-scarred hand wanders the air homelessly,
a rejected offering, it tingles from the red toggle it can no longer feel.
As that taut skin swung through the air, at last its look registered:
both burn tissue and the flush under fingernail polish,
scar shine over a starlet's pinky,
over warmth a cornea of ice.
The boundary between them hazes with strange growth.
Three hundred homeless hang on, some of whom
would have signed on with the whalers out of here.
Recruitment was matter-of-fact. The press gangs
were long since legend and Royal Navy.
Emmett spoke at the memorial where also the Congressman
with a Cee-Aye-Aay service medallion
who siphons two-and-one-half billions annually to Electric Boat
promised to fight for a year-round shelter.
He stayed to jaw with the drifters, he comes from a safe seat
and did not have to do this.
What he cannot do
no one can, stop the climb down *en masse*
to water's edge at sunset,
the *down-going* as Nietzsche whittles it,
with all the light that we are into earth and sea, *Untergang*,
hugging the megatonnage while we preach against it—
the frail tightrope walker keenly anticipating this,
thus fell Zarathustra well before Passchendaele,
through his migraines and chloral, his ceaseless vomiting,
exposed as he was in the Engadine, shelterless
even under drift-thick eaves, wrapped in blankets,
hammering at us for conversion as he toppled from the wire,
for he was the other figures, too, helpless to sidestep them,

and still no one stops it, for such he affirmed:
do not fail to go under, surrender to destruction, plummet!
Through the blue swell rises the black mound
creaming then pouring molten silver:
up to meet us, what we have fed down there,
its huge shine and roll.
The conning tower is only the guts of the ballast tanks,
the head is only the bowels of the heart,
yet between the diesels and the fuel pump
the prophet failed to interpret his own symptoms,
the succubi, drivenness, tedium vitae,
as did that homeless king
dragged by the line to three hundred fathoms
then cast astray between Thebes and Colonnus.
Recordings transmit the squeaks
and blackboard chalk skids coming from spermaceti
as they sound, pulling the line with them,
hemp smoking as it rips through the gunwale notch
rocking the oarsmen, helmsman, harpooner.
It is year four of the invasion as Emmett holds weekly vigil
at the recruiting station.
He awaits orange prison suits for the next action,
a bargain at fourteen dollars each, but there is heavy demand.
Tatooed Queequeg brought his entire kit here and displayed it
to Ishmael on a tavern table.
I cannot be sure of the details: a pipe, knife,
votive figurines, tobacco? A patterned blanket unrolling these?
And coffin carved in bas relief, his hand and forearm
figured with dark similars.
That sketchy inventory, the uncertain coronary of the victim,
the woodcut 1840s, the inscrutable routes of the subs
and webby scar shine luminescing beneath *ping-pings,*
none the less corral certain details
purchased on estimate although at a price.
The story I would not choose that gets written over my head.
The hand stretches its blank bright aura:
Father's hand clasping its secret, its untold torque

clamping him, no recounting of those days to me,
hands on the sheen of the sheath for the first-born nuke,
he, metallurgist, crystal trimmer, stave shaper
for the self-vaporizing beast barrel, its hunched furnace framer:
and so, then, no glowing fingers pointing
to it, to himself, to me—yet just that veil over
his milky graph paper with blue mesh of cosmos
printed by Pythagoras,
shirt pocket brevetted thickly with clip-on pens,
shy thumbs gripped in his fists, will not allow all these to be entirely evil,
an onlie begotten destroyer from a congress of suns,
for though the spirit of this hour whispered, *You must stand back!*
the spirit of the most vast held me in place
tweezered over this glow.
Here, I will be there with you.... I will be there with your mouth.
Submerged or lofted, the hot nucleus
wheels over parchment in the Rothschild Canticles
at ten thousand atmospheres, two men clambering through its rim
to the fusion core, bare feet mated in acrobat joust, their gowns
blown back along their opposed thighs by the blast:
they and a companion break-in artist, a plutonium dove, have penetrated
past three suns at six Gs and are splayed as flat as squirrels.
If he is fortunate, the bowsman
balancing a second harpoon senses the position of leviathan
as a jilted lover angles a certain side street at twilight
and holds his stilled crew, their oars hanging, in readiness
in the approximate, perhaps right direction.
Nietzsche's room tucked under the eaves
was aimed by its end-windows
straight at the peaks.
Even he halted in his fire sermon,
having gotten ahead of himself, something indefinite stopping him,
as the crowd yelled for their saltimbanque.
Whose broken-neck was the outcome
and whose identity remains conjectural.
The hand is a crazed shepherd
creviced in all the high valleys, orbed in miniscule

in a crowd of lifted brown eyes. Prophet!
The hand looks out of ten thousand faces.
Even dried of all rain its valleys gleam.
Two imprecisions:
the acme homelessness of a gospel life,
friendship as the law athwart institutions
in the willingness to be present across jurisdictions;
and then the evasiveness of murder totalized.
I see my confusion but hold to the tension that breathes in it:
my pledge to swallow myself while I take a stand here,
as if the whale saw me through his depth cornea.
The satyr-faced philosopher led young Athenian twitocrats
outside their city walls to pursue the argument
to its end, into the undefined.
Hard drinkers all, and he the best of them.
Bargaining for favors in a love brawl while selling short for wisdom.
In Turin, haggling only with himself, Nietzsche tested the facades.
He found them immune to suburban impudence
and therefore declared the sidewalks to be in earnest.
Brickwork cornices from his major decades outface Thames neon
but not the depthless gloom of the Boat Shed
squaring off high around its tungsten tonsil.
The troubled tribune of counter-revolution
and pastor's son who read the entrails in the birth of tragedy
chose to descend into his conning tower
in the grip of what he had seen while below
on all his screens and in crosshairs awash with fluid force.
Baptizer down the black wave, gurgling foregoer,
and though murder swells, locus cracks open to breathe.
For rosy skin submerges the veins on the back of that hand
while tensing a crinkly gift wrap for action.
Perverse eros prizes the callus and falls on it blubbering.
The borderline, where the man fell, was stitched by his odd body.
The down-going is to the banal, the dreadedly tedious,
whose rejected heaviness hides the *I AM* as consort,
unflattering to *amour propre*, zone of heart attacks and exposure.
Past the rulers, a shepherd no-account from Ascra,
dripping Zeus's penetrating oil in the rain shadow of the eras,

announced *There is another order!* Hesiod combing
lice and dung from his charges, their alto vibrato fear,
through fog at valley's end, through hazed webs tenting the grasses,
to dig in and serve wool-clammy life.
Bush Babylon's uranium dust across his babes, he persists.
Stand down, vultures,
swerve there, swoop-shadow, there! stand down.
The cold strengthens his fingers.
Two bands of cops hire out to Greek justice, lovely *Dikē,*
whose first profession was real estate. A line untouchable.
So here an untouchable has fallen across the untouchable,
the loose across the rigid, the free over the fragile.
The mortal astride the dead.
Will it explode? The dickering consumes hours.
Because the verse line lifts with the plough's U-turn
it coils inside the untouchable. Will it detonate?
Smooth Rosy Hand knew nothing, they gave him nothing to eat,
yet he bore witness.
Standing, shrugging, walking around, he strengthened his means.
Ineffectual? Persistent. To Emmett's fishtailing placard a driver yells,
Go back to work! then Emmett: *We do the real rite out here.*
Two such prescriptions:
the apex placelessness of shrewd resistance,
its homeopathic touch, its *homo-ousios* titration,
same-same in the old doctrine, the smallest dosage for effect.
Why do we go to the boundary?
Why does he walk badgered and unfed, of the seared hand,
testifying to blankness?
Because of the unhoused. The unhouseled.
Because of the changed air and the unborn,
because of the unsheltered eyes
of the unbearably unborn.
And then the cross-haired back wall of mind.
It was their first date, that evening they chose each other
as bunk-buddies, one nestling within the other breathy
in nourishing hairless darkness. Our brochure updates it:
The pace of forced discharges has actually increased. Violence and threats…
An ocean not enough to float it

nor enough to swallow it up, not for old fire-mind,
the web of matter-energy rent and the gash in it furnace bright,
The descent beckons! cry of the birth-doctor Williams
already two lifetimes earlier,
dancers and drummers sustaining his beat
toward June 2nd's debut
of a mammoth nuke surrogate
in the old nuke testing fields of Nevada:
Chippewa, Winnebago, and Shoshone
warming up to insert their own kind of rods into the field
above and below, putting some reinforced concrete
into the faces of earth and sky.
The plan calls for 700 tons of nitrates and oil to explode,
to mimic the slam of a nuke penetrator.
They postponed it. Bides its time, *ponere*, put away on the shelf.
If atoms can wait, the physics of eros
can learn to wait also. And then, zowie.
If it gets toyed with, it will be built.
A ploy is a ply is a fold-in or fold-out. A fluke or a fin.
If it can be deployed, it will be used.
Ticking dust from the old atom tests will snow Phoenix.
So were finished the heavens and the earth and all their array.
Something waiting to go off, and they even tell you where,
yet every street hollows out its sunshine,
the stalker just now vacated the passageway.
Sterling? I have no position in Sterling.
And I am clearing out of the dollar.
Bobbing dancers, glistening, against
a cone with fins, a fountain where rock was, the plumed day.
So was finished the service of constructing the Dwelling, the Tent of
        Presence.
Abishag no abscess of senile afterthought
but the reserve wine jetting out, an arroyo's terminal roar.
The only taste of the dharma is a boundarylessness
found only within bounds.
If you the unhoused do not roof each other with care,
then who, unraftered ones, will do so?

The undeveloped now carry on their broad backs the zany developed,
the house dematerializes around the once-great,
Coolie porteth roof on head and so wadeth his garden,
foot in muck, deep in the season,
while Freeman Dyson, who cranked maths for the sorties at Bomber
        Command,
confesses in age that *I felt it myself,* the nuclear *glitter,*
a happiness at hoisting a million tons of rock skyward.
At least the Soviets used rockets to spray seeds
over the farms they ruined.
The dancers and shamans know one thing:
time will move differently for weeks after that blast.
The code name is *Divine Strake,*
strake perhaps for its Bernoulli function,
the add-on fuselage strip or ripple that improves airflow,
from *streken* and *streechen* and *streght,* in this case straight down
with *strake* as the blast itself, a driver—steeper, sleeker through earth.
As the pegged, caulked strakes on a ship
smooth its slide through water.
Penetration beckons:
learning first how to think like a boat in air
and then like a ship piercing ground:
guts yowling up through the head
then a head shrieking down through rock.
Strengthen the ceremonies.
Either side of the recruiting center
boats and small yachts stand propped on struts
waiting out their exit from winter
in the yards of the big marinas, pastel blues and greens
of the fiberglass below waterline
velvetly vastly featureless, the keels *en pointe*
toeing down onto a stiff pad, raked prows and sterns repeating
that ballerina lift, for she has thrust forward and waits,
her calf hangs tautly in the swept angle
of each fantail, a fingernail sheared off in flight,
its ivory or blue or green infused through resin, now
a sheen between water and sky.

On the Sentencing of Philip Berrigan, Portland Maine, 1997

On Chittagong's tidal flats
tankers and container ships
tilting or splat down, strewn in some titan's rummage,
bequeath rust gilding to the salvage magnates—
the brief bloom of an age.

A trained efficient killer
Berrigan's phrase for himself after the War,
artillery then infantry. Then the collar
on a Jospehite teacher of black kids in D. C.,
New Orleans, Baltimore—

sentenced once more in old age
for boarding a destroyer at the Bath Iron Works
in Lenten daybreak. Torches
of the Bangladeshi ship breakers slowly
sizzle off I-beams, leaving bite-size chunks
of flank and rib cage sawed
for the furnaces—not his scuttling
of nihilism, the smooth gray god.

It smashes before it builds,
his tool *le marteau* and its *martura* witness
brunted often—winter
dictates his wool cap, while our homes huddle
in a chill that bones the novus ordo
sæclorum of mid-July in the Hamptons
and August at Alamogordo.

My core Erasmus, pinned here in my lair
seduously, stays intact,
on both men the same profile,
a hawk's through a chink in the night, its compact
turbulence the sign
that down in I'll not rot, nor dance free of the leash,
but meet thee in the mass of the pile.

   Here stones rumple woodlots
once cleared by oxen: no trace of the browsers
who nudged their pink lips low to them.
Pattyquonck and Ponsett, brambles and vines
festooning a wrecked shambles—
thus Thou barrier brunt God!—though I climb through them.

Lumpy and absorbent through the long ebb
of the Algonquians,
thorns over them uncombed,
their tons of withheld action bulging stents
through those girdles
or aiming a drawdown swerve that breaks out
among the starved and the bombed.
This fighter conned the idols
crammed and moving, but also the descent
whose harrowings promise a dear work.

Narrow steps steeply down,
some packet boat it seems from the 19th century,
risers drilled through for drainage,
here it is, then, clammy cool below decks,
the corridors in no hurry
to uncoil, sheathed in creamy wainscotings,
dwindling passage
and a mirror's deep glintings
at one tight turn.

His was the *Sullivans*,
destroyer Aegis class, whose missiles pin
a continent, tracker balls cueing its towers.
It names five kin sunk together,
rescue having been called off—the abandoned then
standing for all at hazard now, all men
held by all, ignorant or cold, under the powers.

By the time they booked him
his innovations lay behind him: anointing
beside his older brother
with blood and jellyfire an altar of draft files
sprawling a parking lot,
celebrants drastically pointing,
using only from one's own body and back yard
what was being used on others.

The charges were construed
as narrowly as the gangplank up which he led:
damages to property,
persisting in trespass, and contempt. They omitted
bad manners:
before dawn, the rummages of spirit
out on the empty dock, impeccably rude—
not waiting to be greeted.

Merton had warned the brothers:
*You won't survive America unless
you hold to your disciplines*—
no outcomes to count on, love's arms callipered
more and more outward, the back
of a maestro riding the driving presto nailed there
until it gives, as he had given,
himself.

    Knowing, too,
that the world—*werold,* the time of humankind
on the iffy shingle of being—
is simply for the children, though human mothers
have held their own by the throat
in the Kenyan bush when Abyssinian stalkers
in the slave trade were nearing,
and stifled those who cried out.
Pig, tiger, hedgehog, our pitiless brothers.

 The destroyers must not win
yet they cannot lose: the aimed man squirming gets gulped
by what he will not swallow,
hap not to be helped,
its sonar gut reaching the tilting parts of depth,
that thick spin lodged in grounding,
and with the shamed ultraviolet of North
he torches its gut into liftoff
and the whole mass creams breaching.

Hard-won law assesses
perpetual damage with its severe beauty,
but also through ditto jaws
and a cued tongue. So John Schuchardt, attorney
and former Marine captain,
knelt on the courthouse entrance stairs invoking
Tokyo and Nuremberg
while tapping a frame drum—

Nichidatsu's monks
have walked it everywhere. The field it spreads
it drums from the fields it destroys—
rearranges
iron filings to its slight current of mercy,
I go, and it sends back the changes.

    Actually to board her?
whose forging my boyhood fantasy riveted then rode
squally into swells,
seam-welded and double-hulled at the urging
of millennia—tossed under,
scuppers spewing then gurgled, many vanishings
sucking at her to claim her

for their sakes and mine:
I am brash bone at grips with handrails corkscrewing
to the engine room, I am the bucket
of brains luminescing over the screens, I am the hand
with hammer and red splatter
unable to disarm it but covenanting
with beginnings and with the end—

though in fact I have not done this:
have only stripped to my allotment of borrowed
integrity and stood naked, while the act,
the free thing, like a wave
breaks from mile-heaped billows pistoned by
the salt-rumped moon.

And so to the bridge
and pilothouse they went,
gaining the aft gangway before daybreak,
to the heli pad, to the missile hatch covers,
banging the crew awake,
terrorizing, splashing it around,
tracker ball dented, a red mess all over
the panels and levers.

   And yet search is also
a downward teacher, zooming in on string
or a coastline to unpack
more and more length, past the border guards
into an unfolding country,
density's outward—the whole in ongoing
announcement, my limit
coming at me with the dissolving force of entry.

Aristotle's grown-up, *spoudaios*,
tracking *nous* beyond the names while present, urgent,
searching, in our day though not only ours,
not to stand apart but to sweat in darkly joyous
turnabout: sucking it up, drenched while drained, dripping
with the dew of the first hours.

The loud rooms in Gloucester
taverns, their accordion jammers—as in Hamburg's
dockside saloons and the dives
where Brahms played whorehouse piano to win young bread:
I bend close, the student listens
for both our drone and the rare interplay
of gold with tar—an Iron Works bar—then I leave,
inhale wind off the inlet

and track one craking gull,
his tilting glide scrupulous for food,
then victory folded in
as he tucks down rasping one Volsung cry,
wind age wolf age ere world plunges wide
its rough size
nerving the myelin wall of the sky's cranium
and the seabed's ooze.

There is no going back behind
fission's products, no shutting
the empty tomb, no caulking the self-rupturing word.
Depth gullies not only below welded keels,
sinks not only through pitchblende,
but also along the sweeting
embittering gin swirl in the eye as sun uncoils
buoyancy from basis. I have long been aboard.

The Tolstoy of horseflesh and behavior,
the Homer of homesteads
parked out in nostalgic floats of simile,
you are that close: conjured substance, neuralgic
phantasms of the real,
through which spindles the victim, wilting in heat
but haunting every last claim

and the March rains bead from air:
where am I now, rare father and brother, edging closer
by going with the dare
that inserts least force, the ablative absolute
of power, as the boulders of Pattyquonck
pile bracken thirsty for the drink
that they are not in the field of the world, unmet.

   Sponge ice graying white rivers,
somnambulist mist shearing at daybreak,
moss agate's sunken lace—
God gropes unfinished, the book of questions not closed,
and process sheathes a cult
of tom-toms past hearing at the roots of fire,
for the trans-animal
at large and at peace is the shatterer, the shock healer
of anything too soon wise—

silent, adamant, unsealing a fathom-fathering
medicinal abyss.

Shock-shackled life hangs
not from some rock in punishment or buckled
into a casemate, the salvoes
punching closer, but awake at the featureless
clock face of obliteration
and birth flooding the same meshes, murder
and ardor pressing in order
from one source—this, this total breaking the mold.

Ecstatic heaviness—so much that
grazing heads seek it here out of homing need—
slowly yet emphatic,
coming as duty comes to the ruminant hand.
And the dark head lifting
is any in this field, bull or human,
that forages the bending shine of courage
from the will's slivery chance.

I Came, I Saw

1	Allegro con moto	60
2	Adagio ma non troppo	63
3	Largo risoluto	65
4	Gavotta grotesche	70
5	Allegro appassionato	73
6	Pastorale – Estampie – Marcia	75
7	Waltz macabre	81
8	Galop marcato	83
9	Scherzo energico	87
10	Gavotta lento – Pavanne serioso	90
11	Intermezzo lento for solo viola	94
12	Scherzo demonico	97
13	Presto giocoso	101
14	Romanza on two poems by Blok	104
15	Largo – Allegro	106
16	Pavanne for woodwinds and steamfitter's wrench	109
17	Andante espressivo	111
	Notes	116

1 Allegro con moto

12 May age sixty-eight, my waking from dead sleep to dread
into terror, the subaqueous drift of hospital
    Malko immediately took the First Symphony for the Leningrad Philharmonic
    performing it on 12 May 1926: Shostakovich was twenty,
whose trailer was an older man man peering over a dream folio—
Invest in the stock market!—Risk life, babykins! sayeth a wise man
   my Father's age, who drove a one-horse ice wagon
     when he was sixteen, at seventy-six synchronizing automated steel lines.
   At thirteen he stood as Joseph in a living Baptist crèche
   and when a sixty-watt bulb, namely Jesus, ignited the straw
   he reached down and unscrewed the infant Redeemer.
Seventy-three years between the premiere and this our conjunction
Sixty-nine years in that self-contained fireball's plasma
And now it is meet and right to switch off the chronometer
and get down to Moira, mythology, and the art of listening across gaps
   The Market: thermometer wriggling in the mouth of greed's fresh cataclysm
   already diagnosed by Lincoln and palpated by Pound,
     the murder of the one and a strong-man virus in the other
     nothing to do with muh-nee, still argue my fellow paupers.
which his foursquare teacher Steinberg could not do, protesting
that the tempo for the Finale precluded both brass and woodwind performance
and balking at one movement altogether: *What's this obsession with the Grotesque?*
The Trio was Grotesque, then the cello pieces, and now this Scherzo!
   The Market! I had to laugh, then it came to me: life wagered
   as investment in the next modulation or modal shift
Mitya wrote out the parts for clarinet and trumpet and took them
   and their turns utterly cryptic

to the cinema orchestra—where he plowed the piano for sustenance—
and they had no trouble ripping through them. He always heard
    lit arrows on the game board, but the force hidden, *kruptikos*
accurately beforehand what others questioned. *Grotesche, grotto bello,*
    no more predictable than the modulation exam with Glazunov—
    they hung at the door while he was assigned the pegs for his progression
caves in the ducal gardens painted with googly faces.
    Came a long silence, then a Niagara of chords *prestissimo*
In the pit under the cave's silent screen Mitya outdid pianola,
sovereign among styles within the crypt of the new state,
    whereupon he sprang out full of parodies and pranks,
grotto tuner synchronous with the flickers in Lenin's vault.
    The dread leaked from what I had not felt when near death
        for I lacked strength to turn and see it, precipice floating there
        in the hospital room, a haze of morphine and intravenous—
Unable to swivel in their stone seats, gawkers in Plato's grotto—
in the Petrograd Conservatoire, Mitya fourteen, the concert hall ceiling angel
strummed a lyre of hoarfrost. One student invented
    a slow audition of the post-mortal coda to the Fourth Symphony
        performing itself whenever I lay awake, day or night.
tin boxes for their hands holding a few charcoal embers.
And Lunacharsky got extra bread allotted to Mitya.
    This man had read the sea bottom for me, he stays at hand.
In 1940 the Moscow audience for the Piano Quintet
sang the roistering theme of the finale on the trams,
the air steaming above their mouths. Then invasion.
They, not the British or the Yanks, won the war
with their hecatombs. Resentment still seeps from Potomac
into the estuaries of undeclared and foisted wars.

    Once home, I studied the overlaid hands of a man who
    rests in a detail from one of Tstuskiridze's canvases:
    Levan and his wife in their seventies, for the first time
    able to see Western Europe, from Georgia
    for a month at the arts dacha in Bogliasco near Genova.
    Huge rolls of his earlier work with them. And no English.
Grinberg, adding to that bile, calls the Quintet stilted:
This is music that does not connect with the life of the people!
    I finally asked, *Has Michelangelo influenced your work?*
    His translator, the Professor deadpan: *I AM the Michelangelo of Georgian
        painting.*
    Both men sans bravado, nothing more for us learnèd bumpkins.
My Swiss landlady afforded me one glimpse of Furtwängler
while Berlin was still being battered, he seated at her radio
    The canvases had been tucked like Cuban leaf into thick drums for rugs
leaning forward: *Ach, zey haff shot ZAT vun…and ZAT vun*
    which they extracted one evening for my private viewing
But vher iss ze vun I haff been VHAYTING for! Largo grottesco, con fuoco
    the smallest of them queen-size, the largest a goodly wall
    and torsos, gazes elemental yet chiseled, the tints rubbed as into stone,
Furtwängler rehearsing the Berlin Philharmonic on film unmoors his left arm
to float with riverine nuance, an eel telemetried by the gods
    and he rolled up his sleeves, grinning and sweating, then stopped
    and looked up: *He was strong, Stalin. But I was stronger.*
The tympanist heard the orchestra's tone go sweetly deeper
when the balding eminence entered toward them once from the back of
        the hall.
    We had a moveable wall, and every night behind drapes
When someone affects the tone that way, you know he leads from the wellsprings
    I got out all my things and worked until daybreak.

2 *Adagio ma non troppo*

Bamboo forests, apes and great cats, 1925—
Shostakovich at eighteen was hammering at the First Symphony—
   A Huichol *espiritista* approaching eighty
   in the calends of Iraq Seven and Obama One came
as the Western doctor arrives with his notebooks to record dreams
mindful of Herodotus who spoke of *man and the other animals*
   to perform ceremonies for the conquerors, camping in canyons
   wading torrents of the unseen, lone servant to the deep eye.
We name the Kenyan Elgonyi for their axis, Mount Elgon,
whereas they lived nameless in their untampered home—
   February's Sedona—lend an old man the wattage
   for those makeshift sheds in Nayarit—
calling themselves *the people who are here* . . .
I may intone their nomenclature but can adopt none of it
   on a slope under the high swags of power lines,
   for a schoolroom under thunder from dome to rim,
   golden voltage zig-zagging as through a turquoise medallion
   whose flaw calls for a crazed seam.
Waiting for sunrise, baboons perched silently along a cliff
as did Jung in his pith helmet: *Like me*, he wrote,
that primate harmonic none the less reinstating
nothing of root modesty in the tongue's claims.
   The old seeker working down canyon through
   a strew of baker's sugar at dawn, to kindle
   scrub under a rock ledge that blown feathers may siphon
The vanishing of the animals on Elgon

preceded the scattering of *the people who were there*, to modulate into past-tense
    from the heights one of the gatekeepers.
In the blue heights I see nothing but a fine day
    Everything went off brilliantly—magnificent orchestra, superb execution!
    thus Dmitri's mother—whereas he: *They poured filth all over my symphony*
and by Hercules there is nothing I can do about that—
even though Sibelius once took students into a meadow
because it has an overtone, demonstrably
    As for the revolution cantata, there was that boy—had he seen him?—
    shot in the Liteyny Prospekt for stealing an October apple
    which he paints in atonal fugato, an intricate high quaver
and though Frank Martin stopped his lesson with a young pupil
flinging the window open and *dancing offbeat to a brass band*
marching past in the Place Bourg-du-Four
    which to the conductor Malko remains utterly baffling
    as probably to the Pulitzer selection committee
because it would soften the plunking two-beat rhythm.
    The wattage, the amperes, lent from electricity's quick mystery
Out of the dark, tuners of pitch and thrust
    so that in a moment he retraces the day's arroyo
through our Childermas of massacres and prayers:
    for he has not yet misplaced the formation
from the dark into the one lit place
    and transformations of his gods.

3 Largo risoluto

Purpose and elaboration in the back-country of mind
    The state will razor you, your ears between high-amp woofers
    on a meticulous schedule while countermeasures with backbone in them
    will mount as if by accident and crest in resolve
build and swell over nine months and then subside, dissolve,
plankton surges tinting the swell then sinking,
Ecclesiastes by the numbers on a long tape loop—
    only if attention, the puppy's eye on the ball,
    is sustained the length of the toss and the bounce—
morals involved, yes, but canon and counterpoint
shaping the outcome, such as it is, as much or more so.
    all that by nature, morals the work carried out *against* nature.
The Eighth Symphony, after Stalingrad, resisted the general relaxation
into deferred promise—better, things have got to get better
Jefferson's keynote for Acheson's postwar kettledrums:
unrest, skillets clanging? *Take Canada, take Florida!*
    Contra naturam, contra dictum, upstream heading
    every minute, those breathing easier especially.
    Antiphons not fugues work better in browbeating,
    let the rest warble while you shout them down.
The Fourth's coda aimed at the Eighth's, whispering, *You passed the Leningrad
    century*
but also more, nature shielding me from it for months
You came, you saw, you narrowly passed the edge.
    At one pole politics is the cosmic wax rolled tight in a ball
    while from the other heave the long swells, sliding blind,

so that conquest, the kings, the great men, mount as waves wrinkling.
Cannons and canon: entries repeated and staggered
    Japanese and Russian bells push out micro-layered overtones
at intervals calculated to hold the attention
    but were melted down for imperial and soviet artillery.
Mitya stiff-armed fugues at the Conservatoire—*No stunts*—
but in 1950 plowed into counterpoint under Bach's spell
    Fra Bernardino, curious to see the armorers sweat in Milano
      and watch boatmen step masts and mend nets in the Venetian lagoon,
        and hear Guarino, son of a blacksmith, convey Greek to gilded Verona,
auditioning his cycle of Preludes and Fugues
before a panel of guild supporters, guild prosecutors, and the young
    had descended Dante's cantos and then had scaled them.
to be roasted by the district attorneys of *real values*
    When he propounded morals, the rhythms of Dante came through, they
      were like life
(poet at the Library of Congress, to me: *Write something that people can read!*).
    But now the blurry part: out of fullness he stripped imagination
    away, its fires wilting before the standing, living glory.
Lyubov' Rudneva stood up for him as he slumped, head nearly to his knees,
Nikolaevna had turned the pages, he had played poorly, all nerves,
    So they dismiss him. They start bending their bows,
      the tension of my own mind as it feathers and re-aims, flexing
        toward the thick tapestry of passion's targets: for from its yank back
    to its dead cease, the arrow stays hero of climb and fall
and she saw it: ideology was their fig leaf across envy.
Two years earlier, booted from the Conservatoire faculty by Zhdanov
Dmitri found Marina Sabinina waiting there for someone. *So am I.*
The Academic Council was dispersing, they passed by, and Dmitri

started aping the pompous ones, doing entire scenes, fawning, fussy
    meant for a place past dialectics or refusal, penetrating coldly
    even heroics. The transheroic arrow of Paul Klee, nightmare-huge,
    glowing, childlike. And what guides it
    it wears where it cannot see or feel; and what blades it
    is the one part of its extreme body that might be called its heart.
The man who wrote to Stalin to save young Weinberg
and intervened for Kurt Sanderling during the 1953 vendettas
pulled a funny face in the corridors of theoretic harmony,
chin out, eyebrows raised, both ears tugged *Ahem!*
    And this too is one aspect of the glory.
Stalin dead weeks after the Weinberg letter (no black magic).
    Perhaps you wanted to tease forth a potent and also dangerous thing.
    Perhaps you have what you want. As for what goes farthest,
Don't worry, don't worry, they won't do anything to me
TO THE CHOIRMASTER: TUNE: 'DO NOT DESTROY'
    passing each limit, its *through* always passes the last spillways,
Two and one-half billions on any given day
move in electronic gusts over the oceans
    rinsings-away of all footings, ground pointless at last.
    Into death through what your love has carried,
Those are the Currencies, then there are the Derivatives
    only that *caritas goes*, the Friar says,
at rates of profit pushing one-hundred percent,
    love alone goes
    with us across or through, the rest
    is of no use.
Machines reduce the width of the escape hatch to three seconds.
If I forget thee, Jerusalem, may my right hand . . .

So, chirringly and repeatedly, chickadee! Again testify
    Da Vinci's freaks lolling, leering, his mounted knight
in Moscow's 1940, on the trams after the premiere
    turning and yelling—or two-bulbed star devouring
    and peacocking itself across Great Year—
they caroled the theme from the Quintet's finale
correcting each other, happy to be obsessed,
    still they pulse and regather down thumped lanes of the weave,
    loom frame shaking, wired trackers bent over glow lines—
    each lens enlarging ever more assiduously the disengaging
    fabric, high fraying drop screen—
happy to be contesting each other before
the war they believed had just been forestalled, and after everything
they already knew.
That much they had an ear for, that much anyway.
Discipline in compositional terms
comes down to confronting inner forces
    I grope through its flapping weave
    sweat drying,
so that violence against others might be less
than a flooding river. Since the Great War few have chosen confrontation
    to that non-place at last of
    unspeakably unbroken peace.
    Hawkshade, even with blurred focus, floats to the goal,
by leaving the Maginot Line, turning to the rear, and meeting the heat.
As the sun drops hot metal onto the sea it makes no sound
    and sun rocked in the froth of a sloshed bucket
the scorching sight of it the heart's cryptic thought of the trick
that steps through dissolution into core fusion and holds—

    is the same disc as in reservoirs, puddles, or lockets
    left out in every weather.
The minister gull, black-backed, when he spreads
episcopates nearly six feet, cranks down his mandible, and croaks—
    It is like summer and a moth blundering from trees
    as if caught in camera flashes toward the lit kitchen,
    dried flowers basketed up one wall, that uncut trajectory
Don't worry, I won't hurt you, I won't hurt you,
the whole shindy is inside now
    coming home full, lofted, through gates in the rain.

4 *Gavotta grottesche*

'Nuncle! Lear's Fool alone could make himself royal nephew
by virtue of a word. And at the same time
    Leskov's Lady Macbeth turned to Dostoyevsky
    breathing, *I want to dance with Dmitri*
    and she did not mean Karamazov.
condemn the ruler as a 'Nunklehead.
Confrontation was the chequered game board
across which he inched or hopped his pieces
    Stalin squirmed in his gilded box seat
    leaving early with his entourage
toward keen power and fatal numbness.
    personally commissioning the sledge-hammer article.
Confrontation was the steel spring
coiled inside nimble grins and jack-a-napes leaps.
    Richard Milhous Nixon, you needed better hacks
    with whom you could have kneecapped Ellsberg.
And the entire act held up a jiggly mirror
    An opera theater that lets in the low Russian sun
to 'Nuncleskull—confrontation was neither court maneuver
    when Shosty has penned the score
nor battlefield sleight and slam, but devotion
to the care of the quid, sly *Psychotherapeut*,
devotee of the soul, grease monkey to the *grausame Auseinandersetzung*,
the uninvited sifting guest who skips no steps.
    he reposes cubist mirrors all over the proscenium
    so that it is not only shadows that cavort

  but the cut of the light itself at crossed angles
   through the House, Orchestra first-row to the Heavens.
And so: try skipping steps, and the Fool will turn monosyllabic
  Natura naturans, or the way things gotta go
and exit into snowy night.
   Beekeepers' boxes staggered in colors up a hillside,
   Mahler's hot waxes through horns, muted brass,
In the Spring of 1940 Shostakovich
reorchestrated Musorgsky's *Pictures at an Exhibition*—
   ponds planing pale at evening through hanging grasses—
   one chord, one wide chord for the harp waiting hugely in things,
Rimsky-Korsakov groomed, waved, and sluiced Musorgsky
with eau de cologne. My orchestration is crude—
   tilting forward for that one touch,
   perhaps with the period of a brash comet, one loving touch.
Zoshchenko saw in Mitya both Lear and the Fool:
an infinitely direct, pure child, plus something else,
   Slice through a plug of top-grade Havana
hard, despotic—in him there are great contradictions,
   and the floors of Trans-Siberian forests
   send up cold sunlight with steamy decay
   just as the best dark chocolate releases the very best tobacco.
one quality obliterates the other. It is conflict in the highest degree.
Almost a catastrophe.
In March 1941, four months before the invasion,
  I could not move. Whatever I'd once moved began to caper, to heave
  weightlessly, like so much else that others had moved.
  I shrank awake. Who indeed wishes
he scored Kozintsev's *King Lear* at the Bolshoy

with Ten Songs for the Fool, *his humor clever and black,*
prickly and sarcastic, contradictory, complex, original, wise—
    to call gimcrack his own as well as what the trade pushes?
—and there it is, a cameo of the artist serving *Massenmenschheit.*
    No one else noticed.
caught in the pincers of response
    What had moved was the entire basis.
to both the shadows on stage and the sun outside the cave
    And nothing less than that rock is the tabernacle of movement,
a light blinding and transfixing beyond the grotto:
    I clasp its adamant there to sway, buckle,
for all his loyalty to the early revolutionary aim,
    millet luminous through chaff, or sunned wings of sparrows
and all of the best were loyal—tell that to our bankers and Putschist colonels.
    Irony is our chief weapon, Tate writing to Eliot
    but the structural irony of a self-compromising order
He composed rapidly in part because
surge then break-up jerked then slackened his leash,
each spasm of synchronic mood response
    elicits irony that turns limiting,
    ironized justice breeding ironized art, structure to structure self-limiting
followed by clock-skipping self-exemption—
    but even so, the law of the dinner bell holds:
    a regime has already lost its authority
    when the artists withdraw their confidence—
the Ninth Symphony *sans* chorus, *sans* pumped-up hormones:
In fire helmet on the Conservatory's roof he decked the cover of *TIME*
but the first movement's theme is *almost literally Mozart* (Popov)…
    though the clang sounds, certain seats remain empty.

5 *Allegro appassionato*

If I might have what I heard, I should have had the hoard
beyond possessing, and been obliterated. The mind
craves you, sound within sound, so that it might for a stave
hale from the heights, hang in arching outthrows—
without vehicle, from itself cantilevered,
to wake in wine casks and in rock strata, iron berry
pooling in clear liquors. For, shut down, shamed in, all
that is in us knows these, carries them, these cantata,
and will to the crushing out of light cull for them chorus.
You have extracted vibrato from my impassivity,
you beyond the registers, those waterfalls fixed and pouring,
while the breasted dancer's skull-ringed feet drum the stretched
form of humanity, prone chorale, full, unmoving.

    The minds of Patton and Zhukov, unbeatable in gambits of push,
    tone-perfect through long tank battles, fail the long body
    of the stream, flung from a surge trickle through to its delta
without vehicle, from itself cantilevered—
    Wrists, General, even yours cradling their tense riding crop,
    reach from stems fed by that one river. Ends meet at all points.
    Long body and the long-thrown stream—have we seen them?
all the while out of heaviness weaving slumber freshly
    May any be carried by anything less? Here: it is like summer
    and a moth blundering from trees under the dimmer constellations
these cantata,
    making jaggedly, as if caught in camera stutter,
    through sharp stations toward the lit half-open kitchen sash,

    dried flowers basketed up one wall, and the miniature implements.
    It is that wobbling yet uncut trajectory, come home
    mazily straight through gates in the
registers, those waterfalls fixed and pouring,
    gates in the
form of humanity, prone chorale, full, unmoving
    in the rain.

6 Pastorale – Estampie – Marcia

In Mussolini—*Man is nothing*—and in Gandhi
the primal *imago* duplex pushes through, in each of us bubbling
    By 1946 the Soviets hauled whole factories from Germany
    but in 1947 they had only one steel plant that could fuse
    hot-rolled sheet with structural steels
and then we are bobbing in the great river, *storia history Geschichte*
for mere logic and know-how do not forge fate
    and so they flew Peck over to Magnitogorsk
thus to see grid-joins in a grain of sand
    to prep them on that high-temperature marriage
and palm eternity in the asbestos hour—
    before Stalin's ice fell on Dmitri in 'forty-eight.
    Two years he waited, then in D minor *largamente* spoke the Fifth.
—the player across from us takes his time so as to make no mistakes.
Cheated of land by his brother, Hesiod combed dung from his goats,
alert to certain smoothed-over realities.
    Demimondaine, nude life
    couched unfolded, her golden tuft sifting sun.
    Slapping a jeweled dagger beside her
    without breaking his stride,
    a grizzled Sadhu—then came
Levan painting *Aindiyai and Khadzhi* in 1972
when our heralds were cranking down their yells
although bombers were undoing Cambodia. Auguries!
Those three big men among the rocks
hollering like Ichabod Crane

    splintering glass from overhead, night
    chilling her long scream,
    which comes only from those
    breakable enough
    to descend cleanly—
but with their high-voltage heads still on,
one of them belly-down along a high boulder, were
bellowing for me and my kind in this our forest
which has begun to get up and move toward the citadel
    so that the spaces
What is that noise?
    blackest and steadiest
—It is the cry of women, my good lord.
    among all shinings
I have supp'd full with horrors
    breathed as home to all days,
crimes of war and accounts-jugglery a thick haze
yet respectability, even among the fearful, grips tight
    and she stood wakened.
    I reached for her hand, her gaze.
I say, a moving grove.

_____   *

Don't waste your efforts. You're living here, in this country, and must see everything as it really is. (Mitya, a refrain after 1948)
    A visiting card on umber ground means *This World*—
    I am the blank speechlessness after headache
    during the sticky bomb decades, and sticky now,

Shoot the twelve-year-old—or threaten his father with that outcome.
Snipe at the *difficult* opera, while outside, famine.
   and here—not at Delphi the chorus in photo, an O with raised arms.
Happy, forward-looking, that's me!
But the Fifth lifted the standard
   The Siberian Iris unfolds three under-skirts, each gilded Aida
Lower your standards and keep writing (William Stafford)—
(pennant on pole in the attack rank)
   that is, deny your opponent open battle
(yet Stafford did not know that bit of philology—
after Mitya had held his tongue for two years, since '48
  (Oistrakh: *They rang at the next apartment. Since then I've known I'm no*
     fighter)
   and he, a CO nearly mob-lynched while in the camps)
He would suddenly leave the room, write down what he heard,
   Cirrus over the heads of children from Hungary, Poland, Holland,
and return to the conversation (Vishnevskaya).
   in Spartan glades, Canton Vaud, at the exiled École d'Humanité—
   beyond all survey, such a span, yet in all cases inherent—
   for behind freed motion the hand drops or drapes,
   its grip on the thing or tool at an end: just so,
Thirty years on from the banning of *Lady Macbeth*
he leafed through the score, hands shaking
Vishnevskaya had sung it as he first wrote it
Galya, I'm hearing things I've never heard before!
   I fumble grammar and lose words in the new language
So that's the way it sounds! Thank God! Thank you.
   yet remain a volcano at choke.
I was afraid to frighten him. I wanted to console him. I didn't dare.

    A girl Geheeb sheltered from the War at the École, still struck dumb,
    stood with him at a high window, the two spitting cherry pits.
    Passing beneath them, Frau Geheeb barked her prohibition.
With the second attack wave in '48, in the packed Great Hall,
he sat alone in an empty row
Just think: tomorrow for breakfast we'll need three dozen eggs.
    The Headmaster hid with that mute girl
      in the rich cranny of safe violations
That's my family. How stop composing?
No one had read Pasternak's novel (Vishnevskaya)—
    (No one counted the 46,000 killings in the Phoenix Program—
How can I sign if I haven't read it? –No one has read it.
    from cognitive psych to proxy terror cells in El Salvador
      it spread uncontrollably while preachments were broadcast to the peoples)
    master and girl wide-eyed and giggling under their sill.
The *Satires*, op. 109: *An eagle owl am I*
among the ruins of shattered gods
From tailor to poet they know my call—
    Ice cracking around magma terror, at last she spoke again—
let our kids bash their heads against a wall!
    and so loving infraction will find it for you, the lost path
Rostropovich: *We are going to the West.*
    to places not entered before: the spill is
Mitya: *But who will bury me?*
    into initial saying, earliest air.

_____ *

Pismire, mouse, hawk,
startled Frau Grouse,
    Evidence, evidence remains mute—
    photographs, Exhibits A and B,
which shall I be this daybreak?
    and still more photographs
In the waste-piled polity,
    do not interpret
    but finally engorge with distraction.
a luxury of roles.
Gasher and galled want not,
gouger and walking stillborn share commonwealth,
    Aesopian Dmitri had gone to the wall
    for Steinberg, Brodsky, Solzhenitsyn,
their phantom ledger
squaring a real shambles,
    but cynically signed off against Sakharov—
    Aesopian in score, while in life a *man with the other animals*
    crumpling into the wastebasket
    the letter to Tishchenko:
spilled entrails with sheened lanes
lacing the whole.
Grant me the walls
not fallen;
    To lose one's conscience is to lose everything.
    The end of the runway
    coming up fast, he reached for Gogol,
the parceled-out parities
and the chewed flails;

    linking *The Portrait* and *The Black Monk*
    in a double bill for opera
the blown tinklings
of gone processions—
all that arrives scoured and clangs
with brass climax
    unwritten, fingering
    what he had done in remaking
    Leskov's *Lady Macbeth* :
from the stilled orchestra.
    Why should satire exclude tragedy?
Grant me the scorched
bareness, the ***X***.
    The moon peers in as an old voyeur
    from the Late Paleolithic, still hungry.

7 *Waltz macabre*

Witness borne is not to the actual
brutality and misery of Mars
but to his widow, the *sponsa*
    This part means protracted removals
    first of the eye's power to distinguish
    across heaps the occasional face
    then of directionality in the sound returning
responsibility first a dishrag of tears
and then, perhaps, the self-unfolding act
    cricketing low over mud, billows and pauses
skirling over shocks, a shudder sailing
    as from a spiky frog pond at whose far edge
farther than any representation—
    something huge drinks,
    sound umbrageously genitally
    sobbing, tympani being sucked tiny
    as they are stroked, mallet hand slashing,
never illustration
of either the offstage horrors
or the demanded sentiments
whose horns ripped his jacket and trousers:
    the tuning hand twisting.
art of the film-pit piano
whose riffs thrill but refuse to match
the scene taken for real, that smear of flickers
on the mind's flat wall—

    In this part one no longer telemetries the object
    tracing its ghostings and diasporas,
    for feeling has found itself at last
    hanging over the whole field
the art of high dissembling
    and what it apprehends is the manured bed
at full throttle, fake sincerity
    black with age, in which the object
as tactical arc floating between the horns
    will enter again into generation,
Dmitri as red bull leaper between two topless
    to reappear here, on the two ridges,
breasts taut in the sun at Knossos-Moskow
    to give battle.
Live shell whose tonic shriek is the whole show:
    Already the singers shut what they open
get me through this, *spiritus rector*
    and victory breaks off the wing it lifts,
in your style but not wholly at my expense:
    refusing thereby to lie
here we go, dear
    to the speechless who look up.

8 Galop marcato

Rapallo being three rail stops
east down the coast
I climbed the salita that Pound hiked up to Sant' Ambrogio
from his first ménage with Dorothy, paintings and dinner pail,
to his second ménage with Olga, violin and no vittles—
    Were I to transpose
    the pitch of Shostakovich
    who wobbled in courtship but aced opera
    (ambivalence the mulch of certitude)
    into some native thing
and to a homemade deal table in sunlight—
    the art of high perching
the necks of violin, cello, and bass
    perilous to the scribal hawk
until back down there with Olga programming
so as to admit the bow's social camber
in a social art: newly found Vivaldi with Bartók
    a record of struggle like Pound's but not out on his limb—
Small roof, large beauty, but does the best get to write the record?
    yes, read as a hawk reads, but who pulls the hawk to ground?
Ask Mitya if what he could give was his best—
onto a studded gauntlet, ask wormhole Mitya—
    Were I to transpose all this into one figure
    past the sunny deal table over sea
from film music to three-d, the cast millions, the tempo lumpy:
    it would be a bagpiper

    who releases the tension grieving through things
    across water.
I climbed down from their small house, steep terraces
gray olives over green lanes
harboring blue hot turquoise—
    King thumb and finger let a gift go
    down the air's runnels, angers fast atomized
    along its wake, gift that travels
    to earth's pull as gold against dark Nicholas,
    as Louis Eleventh, as Dorothy Day's work,
then zigging paths sloping through orchards
to meet the Bacigalupos for a beach luncheon,
yet found myself cut off part way, fences and a rail line
but then a sloping tunnel, and ventured several hundred feet
staying to one side in trashy drainage gravel:
    and the piper's drone sends it
    anonymously piercing
not his grotto, not his cave by Circeo,
but such is the one moment of encaved feeling
    through the lake's shine—
pushing through from that gone day:
    for where a system cracks
piss-clammy aura around a bright disc
    grinding people like meal
he among our best, aimed at the warsprings of wealth, yet twisted worst,
    there too breaks chrism,
thus a tarred prophet over the slime pit of securities
    and more than royal
pitch-perfect yet caterwauling at his typewriter

    when its ooze trickles
high over the blue inlet uncreased by wars
    through hair that never
    thought of the vial.
Cool stone bore, weeds, soda cans, and one fast car
grotesque, *grotesche*, that stitch in my memento
    And with the Eighth, he showed us that we would not really win
unsentimental earth's wormhole to fresh light
    and that even more suffering lay in store for us (Rostropovich)
thou prodding me chill bore, thou goading me
gate onto bright houses miniaturized
    The old Persian: *May beauty you love be what you do*
    just missing Hopkins: *What I dó is me: for that I came*
And though once an andante for string quartet
came in sleep, all four voices the year of Pleiku, on waking
    Mitya nodded *Yes Yes* and so carved room to sing *No No*
    Father's steel furnaces exempted him, sabered lieutenant,
I could not write it as Shostakovich routinely did,
    from the pontoon battalion on Bataan's Death March,
for dreamed music locates the mountain,
    or Levan hacking at his iron oak: the analogy not exact.
it does not drill toward the meeting from both sides.
    Show light, yes, but make the way you live opaque,
    for you are, as you are, sealed away from yourself
There came with the firm sleeve through that mass
the dip of amenity and ease,
    already you start to vanish, go dark.
the unlooked-for trick of destiny
as shift from penetration to release

    So cradle the creased head of some stranger hugely old,
    for a second sun ruddies gagged stream beds
    and you will yearn to send
    your hands up ribbed arroyos
and the cavernous finds of breathing.
Seeming stymie and detour have led
to none of those actors, not even the graced meal
beside unpacked waters,
but to this doing.
    harvesting the full foisson of touch,
    where you hid them,
    the deep face and the lost reason.

9 Scherzo energico

Before his death in 1975 Shostakovich completed two song cycles
on Michelangelo's verse and phrases from Dostoyevsky's Captain Lebyadkin.
    Every year in Pharoanic Egypt the swollen Nile spreads
    sunned muck pancaking tautly surveyed holdings
    so that, come the ebb, surveyors stabbed their marks anew
    faultlessly because trued on a rim nicked by star risings
Ill, he sang a melancholiac's love and a cynic's wormholes
sonnets versus *Demons*, space then grotesquerie
and his critics wrestle cryptology: nice little grotto or a bad hole?
    Point to peg to point, twang the cord tight and keep moving.
Does the arthritic titan architect breed the vermin *de luxe* of our politics?
    The oaf, liar, and betrayer in my story secrete how many late pearls
    and do I now assay their gram weight rightly?
A spinster to the librarian: *Are any more of John Gunther's* Insides *out?*
He took with him two unwritten operas drawing on Chekhov
    Chinese boxes and Russian nesting dolls, haunt not my cubby
Many grip their tall stalk of fennel, but few are the bakkhoi,
    but grant me the wit to see spindly legs, late adolescent,
    not as puerile but the rasp of rightness breaking through the shell:
    Shostakovich and Sollertinsky on the beach at Storetsk, shallows out half
        a mile
    both swigging from the same brandy and wallowing side to side
for true inebriates sound dour: one hell of a sobersides, Sokrates
after out-drinking all of his pupils at the all-night banquet
and hell-bent on studying the flute as he neared the tape:
grotesque in the agora, grotesque under arms, grotesque in the hearts of his
        countrymen—

Mitya's first opera cubing on Gogol's satire, *The Nose*,
a success in 1930, banned in 1931, no Bolshoy boards—
Formalism! formalities dispensed with, formaldehyde
leather from cowhide, the cowed thus led to hide, from naugas naugahyde
Alkibiades likening him to those pug silenuses in the market stalls
that open right down the nose onto images of the gods.
The straight line enacted with free rigor through miasma
delivers aim without contempt, regardless of the sizzle
    Therefore in the 1932 *Hamlet*, the Dane holds his flute near his privates
    while the piccolo, drum, and string bass pump out *They Wanted to Beat*
        Us, to Beat Us
    the fight-song of officialdom and its new crop of prole composers
    persisting in his 1928 stance, when he delighted Kozinstev on the set
    for *The Adventures of Octyabrina*, having the Hun cavalry gallop into Paris
    to the tune of Offenbach's *La Belle Hélène*, morphed from the Marseillaise.
and therefore supplies one of the two trajectories
which beauty, awkward force, constantly lobs athwart
forgetting, avoidance, and default—its other curve
being the climb and descent of an actor
willing to lift out of Flatland
at the risk of his own hide
    Protective coloration, sincerely: *I wish to imbibe the principles of TRAMism*
in order to come back altered and altering:
    but in the viewing hall entombed in the bowels of Sovkino House
the Flatland progression affords counterpoint, fugue, whereas
    his tightrope act, white silk scarf and soft hat, large leather briefcase,
the hill path, or the spelunker's, tragic and comedic, chromatically
    ended in a face taut with bewilderment—Kozintsev registered
    the wretched screen, filthy hall, puddles on the concrete,

    and the composer balancing across planks as he made his way
        to the out-of-tune piano. Yet when he finally cut loose, wonders—
stacks each pile of chips on dynamics and pacing—
Hemingway's six-word short story *For Sale: Baby Shoes, Never Worn*
poised against the half-haiku epic: *I came, I saw, I exited*
as Levan's panther sets cocked coils against the eye's flint box
    sparking the damp.

10 Gavotta lento – Pavanne serioso

Chip it if flint, pour and hammer if metal
for either practice archaically ordains sacrifice
of part of the background to foregrounding
a lopped finger from *psykhe* for the reach of *nous*
    Vatic and gnarled wails
    inconscient testaments
    to a bitched world,
    sirens loomed and swayed
blood nowhere visible but the cry audible
    through my first years, above unnamable blisses
if only to itself as it finds itself newly
    down corridors in the small domain.
and astringently ancient.
    Force enlarges itself from those it squeezes,
The sagging, pumping swoop of the goldfinch our warrant,
    a thumbscrew's turn raises the great chair,
raw urge bulges a power arc whereas
    Aion, lion-headed man corkscrewed with snake
    is strife harmonious at last, all of time
imago releases an image, leaving it
floating toward the target
neither my coin nor yours but the treasury's,
    and completed by the doll dangling across a chair,
    the aeons far inside pleated elbow and knee,
and the mint is no house that a man made.
    pudges of stuffing trickling from their vast scene.

Gaze at water for long minutes to make out the seal
    Forms at rest, lying across the blast of process
    exhale, their glow open, most in least—
    the lion-headed man walked straight into it yet is free,
As you grow still it rises, and as you spread it presses in,
the knife a pocket spear,
the spear, an air-mail shiv,
    so the sun roars, rears, coils, caught.
But edge is what you embody
    For he is my passion now
bridging raw urge into image
    and again now stands in me.
Newton collating handbooks on old-gold oven technique
and Dante courting her trace through decades,
    Mitya sat nearly motionless
    during rehearsals,
Goethe to the finish line with his unfinished drama
looped with string in a drawer—
    and Copland near a candle
    at his desk in Mexico,
one fine lob whizzing the ears from twelve generations,
    his swimming pen a blur in the photograph—
proving that it lives and that you just might
    hang with this current's polarity:
Find that pebble heavy as the world and swallow it
    whose seething stillness gloves boulders
to trawl its grottoes for the famished altar
    upland-sanded shiny by wind.

_____ *

Paths untrodden then, steps untaken now, *Stillestånde*
In my gang of ten-year-olds, marbles meant strategic *technē*:
if you could get ball bearings or giant bonkers, why then
eventually you would corral everyone else's pile—
   But it saved us, the atoll-hopping, the beach landings, salvator mundi
   and so General Groves waylaid that letter from the scientists
   Truman and Stimson never seeing it, even later
   Secret until Rabinovitch saw Ellsberg's leak, '71, and blabbed
thus it was steelies and bonkers, or you didn't have all your marbles.
   and Ellsberg's father, designer of the Willow Run plant for bombers
   quit Giffels & Rosetti, after the Hanford plant for plutonium,
   because they wanted me to help build the H-bomb
   at Savannah River in '49. I had a Q clearance
   as did son Daniel in '64, going to Defense from RAND.
And so the only decent push past the mortal envelope
is Schubert's at mid-phrase in the unfinished keyboard sonata
and Bach's off a kindred cliff, catching the big wind,
themselves gone while the jutting phrase remains
titanium filigree into night, no longer in time, resonating
   Thus from Defense to offense, knight to king checkmate
with the pitch held at departure, overtones on credit, reaching
   each thermonuke detonated by an A-bomb marble
still with theory through harmony, though darkly, hands extended
   They'll go till they have a Z-bomb Well, so far it's only N
leaving as monitor the tip of the stick at downbeat
   Lovelock, tracking micron trace elements, then the globe, noticed:
   the sciences go on fumbling at defining life.
each first vibration in performance heaves into takeoff
climbing *accelerando* and banking clear with

   Harry Ellsberg dozing off at the wheel into
      a concrete culvert, killing wife and daughter,
horsehair, bamboo, cold-rolled brass, ebony frogs, nickel keys
somehow keeping it up there
   little Danny intact.

11 Intermezzo lento for solo viola

Past these four walls,
a road,
Norway spruce, stacked rooflines,
then the hills.

But try again:
do I wait
trying these limits, or sleeve
home to them? —On
past this glass burst
the extinctions
of stars and men, and their births,
and, unforced
because it goes
unsurveyed
as knowing, goes a knowing:
that none of these

lends a name to
the flame-sound
streaming beneath and through them
as bond, nor to

the seeing that burns
calmly
across them; that light rodding

the lofts in barns
streams in oneself;
and that
space buoys up the spark
of home in the gulf

of appearances
to some end.
And this is what the soul knows,
and what it is,

though by the drum
scattered,
by the sword broken, Lhasa,
Jerusalem!

Heraclius
had come
nine years before, returning
the true cross.
Now his own people
saw him
wait at the Bosphorus,
Constantinople
not far, in terror
of the sea.
They built a boat bridge for him
and screened the water
with palisades of branches.

He was dead three years later.
Across reeds

in the salt marsh,
threading
filaments of a wall-hung
forgotten torch,
the secret: that
the full
manifestation is
what is and that

its images are
where you are though you be
covered, rages
or contumelies
hiding it
in the kernel of your fire;
that the armies

must come home;
and that
I am, and shall come to
know that I am.

12 Scherzo demonico

John von Neumann at pause
while all the others waited:
he ran it down and scotched it,
chink plugged in the rampart of numbers
where his touch fit seamlessly—
So much for that particular problem!
    Reinvent state and class
    and with it opera
    eight years sweating in the vineyards
    for theater and film music—
    But go to Berg, Krenek, Mahler, Hindemith to learn
    And for this the hammer at last came down.
    Evolution, and add the *R*, yes, but keep *Woyzeck*
This was no lay sung by winds
but a glimpse my Father had on the job.
    I too embrace the extinction of species
    but not of *Lulu*
    Cavalli wedged in the aria,
    what might we not do?
And so just what am I brought close to?
March Hare shooting the last chasm
because he has to,
a most generous rabbit at that—
    Leskov's *Lady Macbeth*? Our lady, surely,
    but not Stalin's, early '36.
Yucca Mountain beyond the bombs

shoots just how far, wily
Hungarian and computational hare?
    Chalk horse forms at Uffington
    neigh to Picasso's at Guernica
    but the warthog, snuffling soil, braces to kill
as Qu Yuan flit-fingered frets on
WHAT SHUTS THEN DARKNESS? WHAT YAWNS THEN BRIGHT?
    The Bulgakovs of all stripes (Pasternak)—
    No one will return those years to us
    Cuvier on Paris's fossils: *éspèces perdues*
Even the ticking March hare
was what he was by nature,
hung like the radioactive mountain
    déluges…catastrophes… événements terribles
within a self-sufficing capacity
    Golden Toads in the jungle
for transforming number,
    then speckled ones in my back yard: fade-out
pointing no wind-ey way through the new troubles
    Indeed Shostakovich has a finale problem! Finis.
or the old, or their uncanny offspring.
    Coda to the Fourth, not my own finis,
    coda & intravenous Over and Out, out of death's grip, *sposibo*.
Don't go looking for them, they will spot you
easily enough, *hombre*.
    At State they raged against any attempt
    to make the ignorant and incapable dominant in the earth
in '64, Khrushchev tossed out, came *The Execution of Stepan Razin*
Mitya: *They'll attack the coarse naturalism*

(the dominant rides on the tonic, and the tonic was revolution)
as well as the depraved conception.
    Robins on Red Cross stationery weeks before the Winter Palace:
    The poorest service by Americans is to stupidly and blindly turn back
    You were safe, Melville—*America the Israel of the nations.*
 Appalachian Spring raises a Pennsylvania farmhouse
with a Shaker hymn about coming down right where
you ought to be. Shaking, trembling, sweating.
    Resisting his boss from the House of Morgan, Raymond Robins
    set Red Guards to watch over Red Cross
    food and medicines: no losses.
Shelved Sholomov, did Mitya—*How mask the fact in an opera*
that the hero does not embrace
Soviet Power! That day he read no further.
    So it's no-go *Don Quixote,*
I shed hobbles in feeling Von Neumann
work out the weird sum. It is him being worked out—
    and it's no-go *Der Ring der Nibelskayas*
    and just here
the most sullied of the fathers must turn pilot and,
    you take up pen and
halting, speed trembly across the fissures
    go out into piled drifts
onto ground, the rim
    with nib charged, nose leaking
    and atrial fibrillation
    lending Cuban rhythms
around the table of Heaven   nowhere else
to be curved home than here.

Documentaries of experience
and breviaries of hope
rub and chafe in the corners of shock
with plays of narrow light on the faces of rare kin,
    to the whole ensemble
    by this time skidding thirty versts past
    any known *universum,*
    knowing that this time the pulse rate
swept to margins by the spate
    will take you out damned glad to go free
of the denying current.
    Exploded through space, they assume,
One enters a small room, they rise,
    but now you may report that
the neighing half-panic ceases:
    in fact the palm's life-line
as a trail grazes the last corner of fugue
    squeezes in on all the others
to open onto the lake,
    for you crumple in the fist you invited,
    tiny, the celesta dinging pendulum-like
    as in the coda to the unperformed Fourth
    though known in piano score for decades,
riven fire of a known water
where we stood small…though by then it stood
within us, a glitter of far searing havoc
composed on it and in us
    your own fate, meet and sweet
at ease, staring.

13 Presto giocoso

August 1945, at Ivanovo, the rest of the 9th Symphony
on a wide deal board his friends had nailed to four poles,
    Coeval with Hiroshima I gazed at slag heaps
    still glowing, disgorged from swivel-body hoppers
Zhitomirsky first learned of the uranium bomb from Dmitri
and Nina Vasilyevna, physicist—his gaze absent, face white
but when I lamented he cut me short: *Our job is to rejoice!*
    on a siding in the country near our house
    age four, Father driving me there
    merry as he gestured, this from the feed for furnaces
and the 9th although playful, *at times a sort of festive swagger*
    whose endogas generators he patented—
transforms into something tragic and grotesque (Zhitomirsky)
    An axe can't scratch out the pen but then there is magma
which cuts through the cant rejoicements of officialdom—
    piccolo through bass-drum burps of trombone blague
it was the setting I have looked for
to place behind Father's sleek alloy
for the bomb casing
    If they chop off my hands I'll write with my teeth.
    A tone row sets out the entire array
für die Bombenumkleidung
    but a voice can bathe in counterpoint full-body
containment so as to transform jolly old munitions
    and as it grows can also incorporate the row
into something tragic—

    A crystal-deep sortie among the rain-sign years
       delights in clarity where mist was and muffle,
a packing crate for Ezra in the cage at Pisa
a card table in our upstairs back room for C. E.
       the two strands one sunrise-midnight serpent,
and a sunlit deal table on poles outside the dacha:
       the totality of tail in mouth,
all within four months and only some of it
       confrontation down the avenue of the spine.
among those works *not recommended for performance.*
       For self-same is opposition from the seed.
For Pound rounded down is Beard sheared near:
expansion, my butter not your bread, means war,
therefore key and tempo matter: strike
into tritones, turn inward where the clangs go, build neighbors.
       In *Piano Variations* Copland melted
          episodes into blocks—*to develop means entering tragic reality*
          four pitches, one great depression, *metallic sonorities*
          and that was pre-F.D.R., who charmed the finches
          off the fence rails into Open-Door, open-score imperium
Corporatist state? We had our own, and we had Sousa
Pound rounded up is a caged bird STOP SEND MONEY
     playing Japan against China and both against Russia, *totaliter et tota*
Copland, *Rightness: I worked on each one apart, not knowing how they'd go*
          together
    I must retain complete freedom of action: F.D.R., Moscow, late '44
At the Waldorf in '49, Shostakovich was hustled off
by his beefy guards into the big elevator
after mouthing his obligatory slur against Stravinsky,

That was one freedom Mr. Seeger did not enjoy—
whence Cong. Busbey got *Lincoln Portrait* scrubbed from Ike's Inaugural.
either then or later—but he did own a ban-jo,
the notional national instrument
held up like the cross, still sounding, to end his concerts.

14 Romanza on two poems by Blok

Gamayun,
   Slow hand rising,
   choirmaster and choir
ptitsa veshchaya
ona veshchayet
   gaze at each other,
i poyot
   not yet do they sing—
ne v silakh kryl podnyat
   so again I hear it,
smyatyonnykh
   back-row rattle from
   one who could spare it:
Gamayun,
great cormorant
of foretellings
   gassed at the Somme,
   he sold doilies, knick-knacks, blown glass,
it caws and warns
but is powerless
to lift its shaken wings
   he wore perfume.
   I came to his shop on errands,
   a blank boy. Thus his toughness
(Shostakovich fresh from heart failure, op.127)
   (was it that I was sent for?)

    gave me the slip—

    for David pranced ungirdled

    into the glowing unbridled presence

Taynyye znaki

cryptic signa flaring

gold and scarlet poppies

v nochnyye peshchery   through night's grottoes

    leaping, and Lord

war before me and   *pozhar*

    your scented wind nudges many such

leaping flames

    out of the grid.

15 Largo – Allegro

Sun opens: from life win wisdom,
sun closed: to others in need bring heart,
and there will be no occasion to fear death—
    Bound to me, hung downside up,
      the carcass of my deeds, close rotting thing,
      that in the front room. Opposite,
beneath a broken-backed senior
beech trunk thatching the stream bed,
    my blind double bu-bubbing on a bass drum
    and there were many, too many around them in each place,
just there where lumbar splinters
soften in every weather,
    substanceless, runny.
    And yet, squarely between, blue door
    of air and a fresh sea,
    and swordsman, and queen.
    The ropes had been slipped, and the child,
    mine, hovered in her arms,
    their few things wrapped in the boat's corner
    and wind beginning to take them out
    over the tremor of accumulations
      into the hazes of abiding currents, their sheens.
a host's hearth kindles deadfall for feed's dole,
face to face in firelight the great confrontation,
stranger now stranded with yourself yokemate,
childfather to the uncherished

brothermother to a mothbrave flame,

all other encounters spring here

or crest when twigs crackle

    Junipers spaced stellarly up a gold field

    claiming it in the name of King Promise,

in false life's pyre, the fool's laugh

vaporized up flues of rippling mercy:

    he of the branching oncoming wealth of seed,

    these lone pickets step out stanching a great wound,

singers test the intervals, toasts yearn

Many Years, one spark spires and

the enemy sits among us,

    taking possession: I grant it to them yet turn away,

    seeking what they abandoned, the cordgrass republics,

they divide what is ours, the spoils

    and abundance in the loaded seam of the last mountain,

    the heart's left side joined to the lost colony expanded, glad,

their sword flash will fly to scabbard,

swinging steel shine will sink sheathed,

    there is sorrow to match these, but streams as dust from harrow—

Harali Haralo! Long life—

    enter the mountain's trickle with cold melt,

Haralo Harali! Life drawn out

    to that mate past kiss, kin, pain,

    who wants only your ore and your river,

to length in your overcoming.

Thus the diver: hands and then face

    who precedes you densely yet plainly,

rupture membrane and then flowing depth

    not at all you although straight through you
the placeless heart sliding gut knees in a clasp of foam
    past your groom, bride
the whoosh of entrance neither a fish dark in the well
    and tent of their meeting,
nor slap nor chance.
    its pennants whipped side to side.

16 Pavanne for woodwinds and steamfitter's wrench

From fountains before beginnings…
love song to the All
lacking an addressee
who has heard those waters, and burbles,
    To reconcile more fully with the fact
    that Father secretly crafted the sheath
    for the bomb at Hiroshima—
    containing blast forces
    so as to set loose far greater ones—
though now the medium
sullied with overuse
litters and fouls the pools.
    I revisit the morning he wrecked the bathtub plumbing
    before leaving on foot to catch the train three streets away—
    village at the midpoint
    on the Erie line between New York and Chicago—
Augustine's susurrus:
through waking, stupor,
at every level of the house at every hour
    so he ran to the cellar
for those who did not survive
    with a borrowed four-foot wrench
although not transparently from those who did:
    to shut down the main valve.
dies and comes into being
    Stone walls, jars of preserves

inasmuch as it is not what it was
    and rust; he leaned on the long lever
and becomes what it was not.
    ripping the line open.
The house, the whole house, in that place.
    A cold jet sprayed stairs, jars, rough dripping stones.
House as earliest mouth,
    The gush and gurgle I hear under their raised voices
sure of the fountain's urge, fathomless, bright,
    persisting through divisions, coolly insistent,
though bright not with these lights
    the unacknowledged force, reconciliation.
nor certain with these fading sureties.
    Through the front door running
    bags flying, he yelled, *Got to go now, Louise!*
Beloved with no face we have ever seen—
as when a house stands quiet,
    And now I lay his iron tool in our crypt,
and mutely in it one bends,
    the atomic envelope already
cleans, rearranges, stands
    a delivered fact,
to hear something when after all, it seems, there was,
    trying to use no more effort
    than the big workmen did when
as we say, nothing.
As when and how sweetly,
    they lifted it into place
then as, as there.

17 Andante espressivo

Book of the living, wind riffling its pages. To stand to that, what a calling.
To be on the move through that, what a job before standing—
Eretz halamot, eretz ha-behira, dream land, Land of Choice,
only such a scoured and blown place works the changes.
    Marshal Zhukov and his staff pulled seventeen-hour shifts for three months
    preparing the invasion, ammo piled at the borders open to weather,
    urging Stalin toward a May premiere, who said, *Nnnno*, Hitler was all tied up
    but Hitler, trumping his generals, beat Zhukov by two weeks.
Memory itself there ripples mirage waters, goes to the piled rocks for burning.
    Three years later, plowing aside the wreckage, Zhukov advanced.
    In Oklahoma caterpillars toppled homesteads with cowcatcher plows.
Memory, precise, innovative, vague, ushers in fireballs.
Twelve lanes in Los Angeles, seaward sun through palls from brush fires
under attack by copters and chemical drop planes: no one slowed, no one was
        awed,
    Levan and his wife came down the salita from his studio after lunch
    for their Italian lesson, they would be seeing Masaccio and Big Mike
    in the flesh at last, going from Liguria to the Del Carmine on Arno
they were at home already while aiming there, the vague was in them and
        working,
    and the newly scrubbed Sistine, all those Puerto Rican colors.
slice through an anthill at evening, contrapuntal muffled thuds from the drops
over tire swish, at rest in rehearsed menace and mastery. *Eretz ha-behira!*
    Levan in his suit, Irina long-skirted, behind them the trembling French coast,
    past seventeen, language learning craters, but guerilla surges are possible.
This was the motion the master wanted in his Sistine Universal Judgment,

lodged here while taken from There, that whirling suck held red through gold
among Rahu's rages in those tangkas where his gaze rides empty at last.
 The breakthrough came along all fronts, but they sat tight before Warsaw.
 In their late seventies, translator in a side car, through Florence, Rome, Siena
This was, but it is not over, this is and shall be for the foreseeable. This is.
 yet in seven years, are they alive? No citations in the state blurbs on art.
 The Yanks still claim that victory grew out of Normandy, not Leningrad,
 sweltering in tunic-tight inferiority, dispatching hit-squads until
 an infant millennium's Afghan ridges, and hit-men, and drones,
 the General on one meal daily, his redcoat snipers on one-bullet rations,
This is the hotel, said my masters of the pre-dawn. Desktop register
chained to shellacked mahogany, brass loops afloat on ambers.
This is the last hour of the night, and here be rooms stably adrift by the book,
desert as lake perhaps and going by the numbers.
The vague is in us and working. This hotel is the place to stand? One stands
  just here?
 one down, and one down, Galahad red-eyed, the tribe in rumpled sleep.
Yet not so vague, ache past the meld point,
this hotel is the piled altar, mound where the contract clarifies?
 Grotto of the fathers, black with entrails, proxies busy past the mouth,
 one may sound inflamed simply by citing occurrences,
 but occurrence is the sprint together toward meetings, that thicket called time
 recurring if behind us, concurring if flooding from the levee and leaving us all
 standing around like Navajos pointing down: *This is today!*
In the first room, a friend freshly widowed, over her head his hand
reshaping recollection, distilling it. So every one of them here
is aiming at a fine hard thing, by the numbers. She could not see him, of course.
Helen Keller in the next room, vouching for Swedenborg: *I have seen, heard,*
  touched!

For concurrence is the whole battalion running under full kit through the heart
For to see is to understand. Then Beckmann in uniform as if in field hospital,
    not as time, which does not exist, but as realization: I may not understand
a fleck of red at his collar. *Das ist meine credo—*
    but I sense, that everything happening just now corresponds to itself
a painted hand, a grinning or weeping face—our hearts and nerves we must abandon
    item for item, synchronous not through logic but because reporting for duty
to the outcry of the many impoverished and deceived—
    at one and the same moment—Tighten those ranks, sergeant—
senseless to love it en masse, this collage of banality and pigheadedness,
    which after the fact accounts for Hildegard's parade-ground impulse
ourselves included, yet every day I love the person it brings as if they had just
climbed down from Orion. The sun, browned out. To see is to understand.
    to stipulate that among the nine choirs of the angels a central group
    swells to five, the five senses known to her, our all-weather ammo
    roping the unity of sensing across the Mississippi of concurrence.
Thomas Browne's desk from Leyden only three doors away
where he crammed at medicine while squinting at alchemy, the numbers
    Tick off the order of the day, you have endless upstream marching
not vague but steep, the Third making toward the Fourth past our dualities,
    which composers know, as we do not, how to make run together,
the schools were after something fine and they knew it,
    even though we are deeply impressed by the gathering and survive it.
Miss Keller stroked the loops on his flasks, Klein bottles fizzing over him
    Politics either waters or obliterates this, or you, or the next bloke
curled in his blanket, blown out like his lamp, rocketing toward the vast Fourth.
    for one does not simply stand still, pointing down,
    but awakens, or tilts into mud with the Commissars of Enlightenment.
Uncorroded, the chain anchoring the book. Flotation bags suspend it

and they said this was the place. Night ending, and the fine nests within effort,
flesh inside soul, this puny hotel rises inside a light rolling and rising,

    Those are the Currencies. Then there are the Derivatives.

    To compose with masses of sound, the available weights of earth

    in the clarified romp they afford, ventilates fear—and

plant growing overnight that shaded you withering, and going through a worm's jaws,
and those taken away you could not save but neither did you grow and water them:

    it is neither tart nor *fou* that the soul hangs wallpaper

    or sears off warts and collects fees.

And so, you want to give up? There is no redress, no vindication, all
withheld from the likes of your generation. So, one stands here.
Sort it out for once. Shabbily or grandly for you the glory is.

    Collected: thus over amplitudes of forest in wind-toss

    and seas dimpled by ball-pean sun, all mind scattered

    begins reprise. And thus collected: feeling in its long scatter

    warms and remounts air to a rolling glide of synopsis—

You think the manner of it is for me nothing?
There is no one at the desk, nothing to see, and also I may be hearing things—
yet the fine somewhat eludes the senses, contrary to the likes of my generation.

    appalled, the lamp sputters and calms. From every wind, down every coulée,

    strict greeters of return rise to send

    all cast-off particles back down the ways

    of luminous and single focus, the homey nowhere of terminus.

To see and hear in that way is also to understand,
so the void voice stands, rises and pivots *contraposto*
like the master's Greek athlete
as Christ as Judge, stands lifting its baritonic
purifications among all those tumbling down
from Orion and up from the mire.

    So through the clock drive iron,

        gain stillness past that stroke on the stilled wave,

        the better thing is not coming, the worse behind. Hear space ringing,

        sound rolls steadied from the vein,

        feed, even here, upon the second blood.

Stands as a figure speaking a figure seeming to speak: what stands

    is the wave at hang,

is the unspoken, a hammered span of quiet

through the mute throat of space,

    reprise commencing, the spike withdrawn—

    Ends meeting at all points, it is like the moth at midsummer

the senses all shot through by the shinings of mute love,

    blundering from trees and zagging the constellations, flash-flash

room after room of welcome paneled, commodious, and by the numbers

    toward the lit kitchen, straight through gates in the rain

in answer to any cry.

Notes

My sources for Dmitri Shostakovich are the volumes by Eileen Wilson and Laurel Faye, and the memoir by Galina Vishnevskaya. The source for Aaron Copland is the two-volume memoir co-authored with Vivian Perlis. The glimpse of Jung in Kenya draws on Blake Burleson's *Jung in Africa*. Max Beckmann's passage comes from his collected prose in English translation, edited by Barbara Copeland Buenger.

In movement 3, *Largo risoluto*, "Jefferson's keynote for Acheson's postwar kettledrums" alludes to the imperial doctrine promulgated in Dean Acheson's National Security Council Document 68, of April 1950.

In movement 6, section *Pastorale*, my Father's visit to Russia to transfer steel-making technology would have been among the last such loans authorized by the Western powers. In the same movement, section *Estampie*, the anecdote about the Geheebs I owe to Prof. Thomas Cassirer. In the same section, the phrase *it spread uncontrollably* quotes Alfred W. McCoy on the "Manhattan Project of the Mind," practices already five decades old (*A Question of Torture: CIA Interrogation from the Cold War to the War on Terror,* Holt, N.Y., 2006).

In movement 7, *Waltz macabre*, Robins's role in Russia 1917–1919 follows William Appleman Williams, *American-Russian Relations* 1781–1947, the chapter on 'The Birth of Containment,' Rinehart, N.Y., 1952.

In movement 10, section *Pavanne serioso*, the Ellsberg material comes from Daniel Ellsberg, 'Hiroshima Day: America Has Been Asleep at the Wheel for 64 Years,' *The Nation*, 6 August 2009. James Lovelock on science's definition of life: see *The Vanishing Face of Gaia: A Final Warning*, Basic Books, N.Y., 2009, chapter 7.

In movement 11, *Scherzo demonico*, the adage WHAT SHUTS...etc.? is an ancient riddle from the *Tian Wen*.

In movement twelve, *Presto giocoso*, the materials on *Piano Variations*, the cancellation of Copland's *Lincoln* from the 1953 Inaugural Concert, and the 1949 incident involving Shostakovich, come from both Copland volumes co-authored with Vivian Perlis. F.D.R.'s sweeping reinstatement of the Open Door policy, as noted during the 1944 Moscow Conference, is cited by W. A. Williams, first in 'The Frontier Thesis and American Foreign Policy' (1955), and then in 'The Nightmare of Depression and the Vision of Omnipotence' (1972), both reprinted in *The William Appleman Williams Reader*, ed. Henry Berger (Ivan Dee: Chicago, 1992).

In movement 13, the lines in Russian, from Shostakovich's setting of *Seven Romances on Poems by Aleksander Blok*, op. 127, quote the second poem's first, third, and fourth lines, and the sixth poem's first and third lines, with phrases from the second and fourth stanzas.

In movement 14, *Largo – Allegro*, the initial bit in strand one paraphrases the late Vipassana Buddhist master Sheng Yen. In the same movement, the first part of strand two describes Beckmann's canvas 'Departure,' while later in strand one, running from *Many Years* through the line beginning "to length," is a variation on the Georgian folk song (specifically Kartlian-Kakhetian) *Mravalzhamier* (or Many Years).

www.ingramcontent.com/pod-product-compliance
Lightning Source LLC
Chambersburg PA
CBHW031156160426
43193CB00008B/390